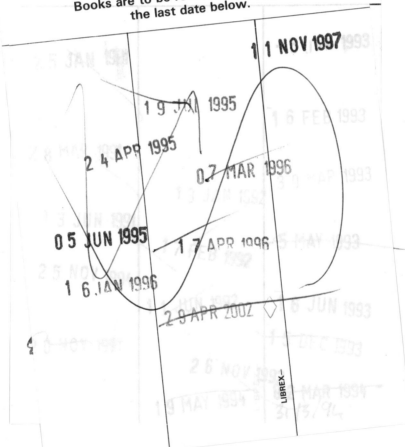

IEEE-488
General Purpose
Instrumentation Bus
Manual

IEEE-488
General Purpose
Instrumentation Bus
Manual

Anthony J. Caristi

ACADEMIC PRESS, INC.
Harcourt Brace Jovanovich, Publishers

San Diego   New York   Berkeley   Boston
London   Sydney   Tokyo   Toronto

ACADEMIC PRESS, INC.
San Diego, California 92101

United Kingdom Edition published by
ACADEMIC PRESS LIMITED
24-28 Oval Road, London NW1 7DX

LIBRARY OF CONGRESS CATALOG CARD NUMBER: 88-83066

ISBN   0-12-159820-9   (alk. paper)

PRINTED IN THE UNITED STATES OF AMERICA
89 90 91 92   9 8 7 6 5 4 3 2 1

Dedication

To my wife, Betty, who has graciously
tolerated the long hours spent in the
preparation of this manuscript.

Contents

Preface

It has just been a scant 42 years since the first transistor was developed in Bell Laboratories, and during that time the technology which we call electronics has advanced at an ever-increasing exponential rate. We have seen the invention of the integrated circuit and microprocessor, together with more and more sophisticated electrical, electronic, and electromechanical devices which are used everywhere from the home to the battlefield. As the array of these high-tech inventions expands, a new and very real problem has come into play. Where will we get the human resources to check, test, and troubleshoot the millions of devices which are produced each day at an ever-increasing rate?

Just as the people who designed the telephone system knew many years ago that there would be a need for more telephone operators than there were women in America, the electronics industry (including Hewlett-Packard Company) realized that some new form of technology had to be developed to partially eliminate the human element in the production and testing of sophisticated electrical and electronic products.

As a result, the system which is called the general purpose instrumentation bus (GPIB) was born. This powerful interface system provides a communication link between instruments that enables the engineer to implement and control, through software, any test sequence that can be performed manually. In many instances it is possible to perfom some automatic test sequences which cannot be easily done any other way. Since most types of instrumentation manufactured today have built-in IEEE-488 capability, the addition of a low-cost personal computer or controller to a test setup is all that is required to implement a complete, fully operational automatic test system.

This book, written in easy-to-understand language, has been prepared for the inexperienced person as well as the specialist. It provides not only the principles of the GPIB system, but also illustrates some of the various types of GPIB instruments which can be used to design an automatic test equipment (ATE) system. Included are many programming examples which are explained in detail. Although these programs pertain to specific GPIB instruments, they can be easily used for other test setups with a slight modification of the commands. The final chapter contains actual case histories, including software, in which the GPIB system was used to enhance and improve the production testing of electronic and electromechanical devices. By using some of the programming examples which are discussed, a test engineer can set up a GPIB test station and have it running in far less time than one might think.

This book will be a valuable reference for anyone who is involved with the IEEE-488 interface system and will provide information which might otherwise have to be obtained from many different sources.

TJ Byers, Consulting Editor for *IEEE-488 General Purpose Instrumentation Bus Manual*, deserves special thanks for his role in initiating this project and using his considerable experience to guide it to its successful completion.

— Anthony J. Caristi

Chapter 1

The General Purpose Instrumentation Bus

INTRODUCTION

This book provides a complete description of the fundamentals of the IEEE-488 interface system, which is commonly referred to as the General Purpose Instrumentation Bus (GPIB). It will provide full technical details, written in easy-to-understand language, to the first-time system user or technician, as well as be a valuable reference to the professional GPIB system designer or programmer.

The IEEE-488 interface system has been carefully designed to provide an integration of one or more instruments to a computer or controller, which allows two-way communication, to simplify and automate the testing of any electric, electronic, or electromechanical device in production, now or in the future. Since it is a design philosophy as well as an interface system, it greatly simplifies the role of the test engineer in the design and implementation of automatic test equipment (ATE). It has been designed with the necessary flexibility to accommodate a growing number of all types of electronic instruments which are being manufactured today and tomorrow.

The IEEE-488 interface is a digital system in which up to 15 instruments or devices may communicate with each other, under control of a master unit, when connected together in parallel using specially designed cables and connectors referred to as the "bus." Supervision of the system is provided by a master unit, called the controller, which is usually either a common personal computer or a dedicated bus controller. The software that is required by the system can be easily written by anyone who is familiar with the BASIC computer language, or is obtainable from many sources which provide a multitude of universal programming packages.

Since modern-day IEEE-488 bus controllers provide the necessary protocol, an IEEE-488 system can be set up and run using a few user-friendly software commands. This allows a first-time user to be able to design a simple system in little more time than it would take with a manual test setup. These basic commands, as well as the more complex, are explained in detail in the chapters to follow.

HISTORY

In September 1965 the Hewlett-Packard Company, Palo Alto, California, began to investigate the possibility of interfacing any and all of its future instruments with each other. It was obvious that the level of sophistication of electronics technology was advancing at such a rate that more complex and superior test instrumentation would soon be commonplace. As new instruments were developed, it became clear that in many test situations it would be almost impossible to train sufficient numbers of production personnel to properly operate these instruments to their fullest capability. As each new type of test instrument or device was added to the arsenal available to the test engineer, the number of tests which could be performed, and their complexity, increased at an exponential rate.

In order to partially eliminate the human element in the ever more complex test setups, some form of communication was needed so that one instrument could "talk" to another and vice versa. That was the beginning of what was originally called the Hewlett-Packard interface bus, more commonly referred to as HP-IB.

A newly formed group called the International Electrotechnical Commission (IEC) took the initial efforts of Hewlett-Packard Company as a starting proposal for an interface system. In September 1974 this proposal was approved for balloting by the IEC. In April 1975 the Institute of Electrical and Electronic Engineers (IEEE) published a document known as IEEE-488/1975, entitled "Digital Interface for Programmable Instrumentation." This contained the electrical, mechanical, and functional specifications of an American standard interface system. In January 1976 the American National Standards Institute (ANSI) published an identical standard called MC1.1.

In November 1978 the IEEE-488 document was revised, primarily for editorial classification and addendum, and the new document was identified as IEEE 488-1978. This document has been the standard for the general-purpose instrumentation bus (GPIB) which has been adopted by hundreds of manufacturers all over the world. More than 40,000 copies of the IEEE-488 document have been distributed to more than 250 manufacturers in 14 or more countries. It is estimated that there are more than 4000 products which use the GPIB byte serial, bit parallel interface system for automatic or semiautomatic testing.

IEEE-488.2

When the IEEE-488 standard was adopted in 1975, designers and users were able to use the system, but not without many problems which they were forced to solve. Because the IEEE-488 document had purposely left some problems unsolved, it was up to the users to determine which instruments would function with the controller, and each other, as required. It soon became apparent that each manufacturer handled message protocol and data handling differently.

A first attempt to standardize the data formats resulted in the creation of a document called "IEEE 728, Recommended Practice for Code and Format Conventions for use With IEEE 488-1978." The formats which were recommended had evolved over time and had worked well with the interface system. This helped provide the information which would later be included in the next major revision of the IEEE-488 document.

In June 1987 the IEEE approved a new standard for programmable instruments and devices. This was called IEEE Standard 488.2-1987 Codes, Formats, Protocols, and Common Commands. The original document, IEEE 488-1978, was retitled IEEE-488.1 The new standard works with, and enhances, the original one. Some of the issues which IEEE-488.2 addresses are:

1. A required minimum set of IEEE-488.1 capabilities
2. Reliable transfer of messages between a talker and listener
3. Precise syntax in those messages
4. A set of commands which would be useful in all instruments
5. Common serial poll status reporting
6. Synchronizing programming with instrument functions
7. Automatic address assignments

The IEEE-488.2 standard was designed to make the interface system easier to use by requiring that all devices provide certain capabilities such as talk and listen, respond to device clear commands, and be capable of service requests. Although other functions such as parallel poll and device trigger are left optional with the instrument manufacturer, IEEE-488.2 requires that when these functions are implemented, they provide a minimum capability level.

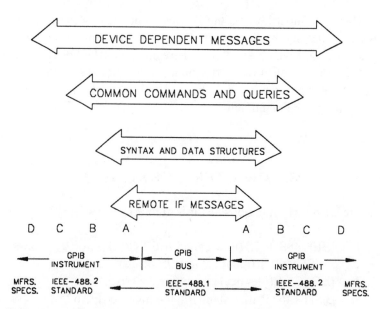

Figure 1-1.   GPIB structure illustrating the IEEE-488.1 and 2 standards.

Figure 1-1 illustrates how the IEEE-488.2 standard works with the existing standard IEEE-488.1. The interface system can be divided into several functional layers, with the lowest layer being the Remote Interface Messages layer or the IEEE-488.1 bus. The function of this section includes the mechanical aspects such as the cable and connectors, the electrical specifications, and the handshake function.

The next two layers are defined by the new IEEE-488.2 standard. These consist of the Syntax and Data Structures layer and the Common Commands and Queries layer. The Syntax and Data Structures layer defines how data is transmitted between devices by specifying the usage of the ASCII (American Standard Code for Information Exchange) character set for data representation. Included in this specification is the data format for binary numbers.

The uppermost layer is the Device Dependent Messages layer which is defined by the manufacturer of the instrument or device. The messages which are defined here are also called device commands; they control the performance and functions of the GPIB device in accordance with the requirements of the device as specified by the manufacturer.

MAJOR INTERFACE SYSTEMS

There are now four major standards of interface systems. They are:

1. IEEE 488-1978 (now called IEEE 488.1)
2. ANSI MC1.1 (identical to IEEE 488.1)
3. IEC 625.1 (identical except for the connector)
4. B.S. 6146 (British standard, identical to IEC 625.1)

Today the most widely used interface system is the IEEE-488, and it is implemented in several brand versions: HP-IB, GPIB, IEEE Bus, ASCII Bus, and Plus Bus. For all practical purposes IEEE-488, HP-IB, and GPIB are used synonymously. This book will use these terms interchangeably, and they can be considered to be identical.

Today, all manufacturers of test equipment must provide GPIB capability to remain competitive. Any instrument which does not contain this capability is limited in its application and may be noncompetitive in the vast world of electronic test instrumentation. This must be considered by test engineers and those who are involved with production testing of electronic or electromechanical instruments and devices. The use of an interface system must be considered at the onset of a testing program to increase efficiency, reduce costs, and help eliminate errors on the production line.

DESCRIPTION OF THE IEEE-488 (GPIB) INTERFACE SYSTEM

In the GPIB interface system three categories of instruments or devices are used. These are talkers, listeners, and controllers. A talker is a unit which is able to transmit on the bus pertinent measurement data or information concerning its status, either asynchronously or in response to a command from the controller. There can be only one active talker on the bus at any given time. Some examples of talkers are voltmeters, frequency counters, and tape readers. Talkers are generally listeners as well. A listener is a device which can receive commands and data when addressed and may or may not be capable of the talk function. There can be up to 14 active listeners simultaneously on the bus. Examples of listener devices which usually have no talk capability are printers, display devices, and programmable power supplies.

The controller is the brains of the system; it provides the commands (through its programming and software) that cause each and every instrument and device on the bus to perform its task. The controller is usually both a talker and listener. The ubiquitous personal computer can perform very satisfactorily as an IEEE-488 controller if it is so equipped. There are several dedicated IEEE-488 controllers, one of which is the Fluke model 1722A Instrument Controller.

Any instrument or device on the bus can be both a talker and listener (but not simultaneously). In any given interface system there can be only one active controller, but it is possible for a very complex interface system to have several controllers. In such cases one of these is specified as the master controller and it will determine which unit will be in control of the bus at any given time.

It is not necessary for an interface system to have a controller. A minimum GPIB system consists of a single talker and single listener, with no controller. An example of such a system would be

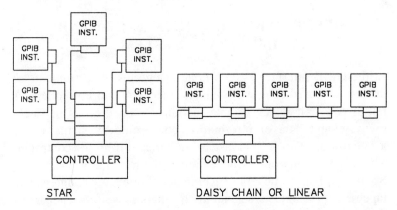

Figure 1-2.   Two methods of interconnecting GPIB instruments into a system.

a voltmeter (talker) and a printer (listener). This system would periodically assimilate voltage readings and provide hard copy of them.

All instruments on the interface bus are connected in parallel to each other by means of an IEEE-488 cable containing 16 active wires that are terminated at each end in a specially designed hermaphrodite connector. This allows a group of instruments to be connected together in either a "star" or "daisy chain" configuration as illustrated in Figure 1-2.

Part of the IEEE-488 document includes the specifications for the connectors which must be used to interconnect all devices and instruments. Figure 1-3 illustrates the pin-out diagram of this ribbon-type connector, which contains 24 pins and constructed so that it contains both a male and female connector, similar to the arrangement which may be found on Christmas tree light sets. The purpose of this arrangement is to allow connectors to be stacked on top of each other so that in a given test setup all devices can be physically located in close proximity to each other. The male/female design of the connectors also permits interconnection of all units in the daisy chain or linear configuration. In any test

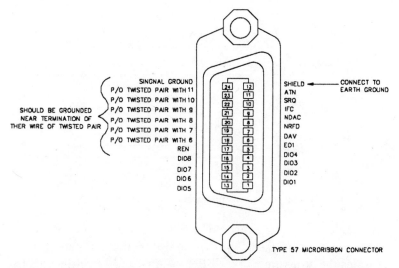

Figure 1-3.   IEEE 488 connector showing the identity of the pin connections.

setup, there will always be at least one connector available which can be used to add an additional instrument to the setup, if necessary.

The IEEE-488 specification permits up to 15 devices to be connected together in any given setup, including the controller if it is part of the system. The maximum length of the bus network is limited to 20 meters total transmission path length. It is recommended that the bus be loaded with at least one instrument or device every 2 meter lengths of cable. If, under certain conditions, it is necessary to exceed the maximum permitted length of 20 meters, this limit may be increased by the use of IEEE-488 extenders. These devices contain active circuitry which can handle the added capacitance and inductance of long IEEE-488 cable lengths.

The cable, or "bus," which connects all instruments of the interface system in parallel with each other contains 16 active wires. Of these, eight are used for data transmission in a bit parallel, byte serial format. The remaining eight wires provide interface and

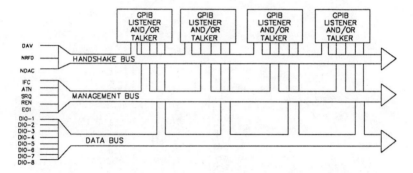

Figure 1-4.   General purpose instrumentation bus structure.

communication management. The bus is a two way communications channel, and data flows in both directions. Figure 1-4 illustrates the structure of the IEEE-488 bus and identifies the 16 connections of the interconnecting cable.

GPIB ADDRESSING

Since the bus is a "party line" type of communications channel, each instrument must be assigned a unique address so that any message or data transmitted by any device on the bus is accepted by only its intended recipient. A total of 31 addresses, called primary addresses, are available and these are usually selected for each instrument or device by means of a set of switches or jumpers located at the rear or inside the device. Figure 1-5 illustrates a typical set of address switches which usually may be found at the rear of an instrument which has IEEE-488 capability.

The address, 0 through 30, to which an instrument is set is determined by the decimal equivalent of the 5 binary bits represented by the switch or jumper positions. The switches or jumpers have a weight of 1, 2, 4, 8, and 16; therefore, the sum of the weights

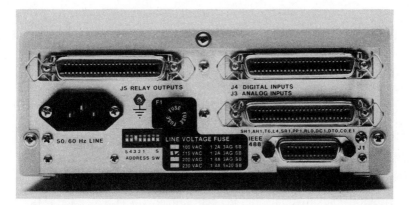

Figure 1-5.   Typical rear panel of GPIB instrument. Courtesy of ICS Electronics Corp.

of all selected switches or jumpers becomes the GPIB address of the unit. Any address number from 0 to 30 is valid; address number 31 is reserved for control purposes and must not be used. Address 21 is usually reserved for the controller talk/listen address and is not recommended to be used for an instrument address. Every instrument or device which is part of a given interface system must be assigned its own unique address number and this cannot be shared by any other instrument on the bus.

Some instruments or devices may also require a secondary address which provides access further into the unit itself. Secondary addresses are usually preset at the factory, but may be changed in the field by rewiring a set of jumpers inside the device. It is permissible to duplicate secondary addresses on two or more instruments which are part of the same interface system. GPIB devices which are capable of accepting a secondary address command are called extended listeners and/or talkers.

The primary address which is selected by the user will actually specify two corresponding address codes on the data lines. These are called the talk address and listen address, and the sixth and seventh bits of the data byte are used to distinguish between the two. Figure 1-6 is an IEEE-488 code chart which illustrates the talk and listen ASCII address characters for all valid address codes.

It is usually not necessary to specify the individual talk or listen characters when programming commands, since most controllers in use today will automatically configure the sixth and seventh bits. A simple command such as OUTPUT 703 in HP BASIC, for example, will instruct the device with primary address 03 to listen. The command ENTER 703 will instruct that same device to talk. In this example, 7 as part of the address code is required by a typical Hewlett-Packard controller in accordance with a select code which can be physically set on an interface card located within the computer or plug-in interface. Select codes can come into play when there is more than one controller in the interface system.

Some GPIB devices (such as plotter/printers) may have more than one talk or listen address (multiple addresses), and these devices typically use fewer than the usual five bits to select the address. For example, if the bit 1 (binary weight) switch was omitted on a device, a single setting of the remaining four switches would select two addresses which are consecutive, such as 8 and 9 or 14 and 15.

Do not confuse multiple addresses with a secondary address. Each multiple address in a device is a primary address and must be treated as such in the software commands. To access a secondary address in a device the controller must first transmit the primary address, then the secondary, usually separated by a colon or comma.

GPIB COMMUNICATIONS

The GPIB is a two-way communications channel which carries data and bus management information on a total of 16 wires, and it is organized using 8 binary bits grouped into bytes which are called

GPIB ADDRESS	SWITCH NO. 5	4	3	2	1	ADDR. CHAR. TALK	LISTEN
00	0	0	0	0	0	@	SP
01	0	0	0	0	1	A	!
02	0	0	0	1	0	B	"
03	0	0	0	1	1	C	#
04	0	0	1	0	0	D	$
05	0	0	1	0	1	E	%
06	0	0	1	1	0	F	&
07	0	0	1	1	1	G	'
08	0	1	0	0	0	H	(
09	0	1	0	0	1	I	)
10	0	1	0	1	0	J	*
11	0	1	0	1	1	K	+
12	0	1	1	0	0	L	,
13	0	1	1	0	1	M	−
14	0	1	1	1	0	N	.
15	0	1	1	1	1	O	/
16	1	0	0	0	0	P	0
17	1	0	0	0	1	Q	1
18	1	0	0	1	0	R	2
19	1	0	0	1	1	S	3
20	1	0	1	0	0	T	4
21	1	0	1	0	1	U	5
22	1	0	1	1	0	V	6
23	1	0	1	1	1	W	7
24	1	1	0	0	0	X	8
25	1	1	0	0	1	Y	9
26	1	1	0	1	0	Z	:
27	1	1	0	1	1	[	;
28	1	1	1	0	0	\	<
29	1	1	1	0	1	]	=
30	1	1	1	1	0	^	>
31	1	1	1	1	1	—	?

Figure 1-6.   GPIB address chart showing the address switch positions required for each address, and the ASCII characters for the TALK and LISTEN addresses.

words. Data and address information is carried on the data input/output lines which are identified as DIO-1 through DIO-8. Of the remaining eight wires, three are used for the handshake function and the last five provide system control and management.

The GPIB uses a negative logic system which specifies a zero logic level on any line which is "true." Conversely, any line which is open has a logic level of 1 and is defined as "not true," or "false." An important reason for this negative logic convention is to allow GPIB devices to be designed with transistor open collector output circuits which pull the lines to zero voltage level to indicate a true condition. Using this system, it is possible to connect all devices on the bus in parallel, and any one is thus capable of creating a true condition by its open collector transistor driver. Additionally, the negative logic convention reduces noise susceptibility in the true state and provides a not true, or logic 1, state on any line which is not in use or is disconnected.

Messages and data are asynchronously transferred over the bus in a byte serial, bit parallel format using an interlocking three-wire handshake technique. This ensures data integrity in a multiple listener system where the data acceptance of each listener can take place at widely different rates. A two-wire handshake system could allow multiple acceptance of the same ASCII character in the fast listener as the slower listeners were still assimilating data.

The maximum data transfer rate is 1 megabyte per second over limited distances. Using the full transmission path limits the rate to about 250 or 500 kilobytes per second. However, since the system is always limited by the acceptance rate of the slowest addressed listener, the actual data transmission rate in any given system may be much less.

Data is transferred from device to device over the bus using the eight bidirectional data lines. Normally a 7-bit ASCII code is used. The international equivalent to this is the 7-bit International Standards Organization (ISO) code. Figure 1-7 illustrates the byte serial, bit parallel sequence when transmitting the message "GPIB."

With various software techniques, other methods to compress information on the data lines may be employed, which will greatly enhance the speed with which data may be transferred. Some types of data, such as transfer of oscilloscope waveform information, require enormous amounts of information. More efficient methods

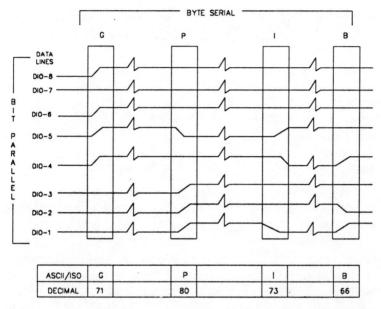

Figure 1-7.   "GPIB" sequence as transmitted in bit parallel, byte serial format.

of transmitting this data will improve the operating characteristics of the bus.

HANDSHAKE

The purpose of the handshake function in the GPIB interface system is to ensure that all messages transmitted on the bus are properly received by the addressed listeners. Many of the command messages which are used are intended to be received by more than one listener, and before any new messages can be initiated, each listener must acknowledge that it has properly received the message addressed to it. The GPIB system uses a three-line handshake, which was selected over previous systems that used just two lines.

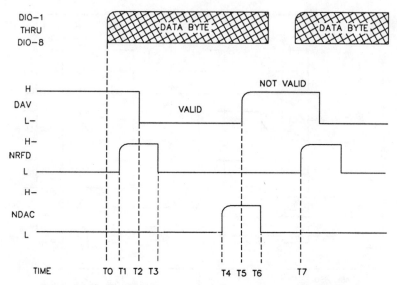

Figure 1-8.   Timing diagram of the handshake sequence.

A three-wire system prevents multiple acceptance of data by a fast listener while a slow one is busy accepting the message.

Figure 1-8 illustrates the functions of the handshake lines as a data byte is transmitted and accepted by all addressed listeners on the bus. The three handshake lines which control the data transfer are:

1.   NRFD (not ready for data). This line is used by all devices on the bus to indicate their conditions of readiness to accept a data transmission. If any instrument is not ready to receive data for any reason, it will pull the NRFD line low, indicating a true condition and inhibiting the controller (or any other talker on the bus) from transmitting. Only when all devices on the bus release this line so that its logic level is 1 will a data transmission be permitted.

2.   DAV (data valid). This line is used by the source of data (talker) to indicate that the eight data lines are settled and valid. The DAV line does not become true (logic level zero) until the NRFD line has been released by all devices and allowed to assume a logic 1 level.

3.   NDAC (no data accepted). The addressed listener(s) on the bus will set the NDAC line low (true) to indicate that it has not yet accepted the data. When the data is accepted, the NDAC line is released. If more than one listener is required to accept data, each will hold the line low until it does. When the slowest listener on the bus has finally accepted the data, the NDAC line is released and goes to the logic 1, or false, condition.

The following is a summary of the handshake sequence as illustrated in Figure 1-8, shown from time zero (T0) to T7:

- T0. The source (talker) checks for listeners and places a data byte on the DIO 1 through DIO 8 lines.
- T1. As all listeners become ready for the data, each releases the NRFD line so that it goes high with the slowest listener.
- T2. The source validates the data by pulling the DAV line low.
- T3. The first acceptor sets the NRFD line low, indicating that it is not ready for the next byte to follow.
- T4. When the slowest acceptor receives and accepts the data, it releases the NDAC line to indicate that all listeners on the bus have accepted the data.
- T5. The DAV line goes high to indicate that the data is no longer valid. The data may then change to form the next byte.
- T6. The first acceptor sets the NDAC line low in preparation to receive the next valid byte.
- T7. NRFD goes high with the slowest acceptor and the cycle is repeated.

When sending addressed commands, the interface message consists of the primary address of the intended acceptor, followed by the interface function. During this sequence the attention line is true so that the listeners accept the information on the bus as either an address or command.

The interface message can also contain a third element, called a device dependent command, which programs the receiving instrument to assume a certain condition or perform a certain function. For example, a voltmeter could be programmed to read dc volts or a frequency counter could be told to take a frequency reading.

Many typical commands to instruments and devices contain a group of characters and digits called a string. The acceptor receives the command, character by character, using the handshake function to acknowledge that it has properly received what was sent.

Chapter 2

IEEE-488 Protocol

In the IEEE-488 interface system there is a bidirectional flow of commands and data between the controller and interconnected devices. Communications between these units is achieved by sending and receiving a series of messages via the 16 lines of the bus. There are two basic categories of messages: interface and device dependent.

Interface messages are used to manage the bus and are called commands. They instruct the listeners and talkers in the system to assume a desired mode. These commands are used to initialize the bus, for setting devices to remote or local operation, to instruct devices to listen, unlisten, talk, untalk, and for other functions which may be required.

DEVICE-DEPENDENT MESSAGE UNITS

Device-dependent message units (sometimes referred to as data) contain the information that a GPIB device is to transmit on the bus and are not commands. For example, a voltmeter may have stored a reading in its buffer, and a command from the controller would instruct the meter to transmit it so that it can be stored in the controller's memory for further processing. Data assimilated by the controller could be sent to a printer which would then produce a hard copy. A digitizing oscilloscope may have stored the shape of a complex waveform to be later reproduced on the controller CRT. In short, device dependent message units are the data which is transmitted on the eight data I/O lines of the interface bus when the ATN line is false and the active talker is sourcing data to all active listeners.

Normally a 7-bit ASCII code (Figure 2-1) is used, but the manufacturer of a GPIB device is free to use any other encoding technique to compress information on the eight lines. Even when such standard formats as pure binary or BCD are used, the sequence between the least and most significant bits could be different for two manufacturers.

An amendment to the IEEE-488 standard, called IEEE-P981, may provide some standardization among the various manufacturers of GPIB instruments. This amendment establishes a common message structure and defines control protocol procedure.

INTERFACE FUNCTIONS

The IEEE-488 document specifies a total of 11 interface functions which can be implemented in any GPIB device. It is not necessary for all to be designed into an instrument; the manufacturer of that device is free to use as many or few as needed for the device to perform its intended function. Each interface function is identified by a mnemonic, which is a one- to three-letter word used to describe a particular capability. A brief description of each function is described in Table 2-1, and is covered in detail in Chapter 5.

In addition to the 11 basic interface capabilities illustrated in Table 2-1, the IEEE-488 document also describes in detail subsets of all functions. Each subset is identified by assigning a number

ASCII/ISO & IEEE CODE CHART

BITS B4 B3 B2 B1	CONTROL		NUMBERS SYMBOLS		UPPER CASE		LOWER CASE	
0 0 0 0	NUL	DLE	SP	0	@	P	`	p
0 0 0 1	SOH	DC1	!	1	A	Q	a	q
0 0 1 0	STX	DC2	"	2	B	R	b	r
0 0 1 1	ETX	DC3	#	3	C	S	c	s
0 1 0 0	EOT	DC4	$	4	D	T	d	t
0 1 0 1	ENQ	NAK	%	5	E	U	e	u
0 1 1 0	ACK	SYN	&	6	F	V	f	v
0 1 1 1	BEL	ETB	'	7	G	W	g	w
1 0 0 0	BS	CAN	(	8	H	X	h	x
1 0 0 1	HT	EM	)	9	I	Y	i	y
1 0 1 0	LF	SUB	*	:	J	Z	j	z
1 0 1 1	VT	ESC	+	;	K	[	k	{
1 1 0 0	FF	FS	,	<	L	\	l	:
1 1 0 1	CR	GS	−	=	M	]	m	}
1 1 1 0	SO	RS	.	>	N	^	n	~
1 1 1 1	SI	US	/	?	O	−	o	RUBOUT (DEL)
	ADDRESSED COMMANDS	UNIVER. COMMANDS	LISTEN ADDRESSES		TALK ADDRESSES		SECONDARY ADDRESSES OR COMMANDS	

Figure 2-1. ASCII code chart illustrating values for bits 1 through 7 of a data byte.

(from zero up) after the mnemonic. For example, there are nine subsets of Talker (T) which are identified as T0 through T8. Subsets of interface functions are discussed in Chapter 5.

INTERFACE MANAGEMENT LINES

In addition to the handshake lines there is a total of five general interface management lines which are used to provide an orderly flow of commands and data through the interface. These lines are:

Table 2-1.   Interface Functions.

Interface Function	Mnemonic	Description
Talker (Extended Talker)	T (TE)	Device must be able to transmit
Listener (Extended Listener)	L (LE)	Device must receive commands and data
Source Handshake	SH	Device must properly transfer a multiline message
Acceptor Handshake	AH	Device must properly receive remote multiline messages
Remote/Local	RL	Device must be able to operate from front panel and remote information from bus
Service Request	SR	Device can asynchronously request service from the controller
Parallel Poll	PP	Upon controller request device must uniquely identify itself if it requires service
Device Clear	DC	Device can be initialized to a pre-determined state
Device Trigger	DT	A device function can be initiated by the talker on the bus
Controller	C	Device can send addresses, universal commands, address commands, and conduct polls
Drivers	E	This code describes the type of electrical drivers in a device

Attention, Interface Clear, Remote Enable, Service Request, and End Or Identify. The mnemonic identification for these lines and a brief description of each is as follows:

1.   ATN. This line must be monitored by all devices on the bus and respond to it within 200 nanoseconds. Its purpose is to place the interface in the command mode when true, and

data mode when not true, or false. When the bus is in the command mode, all devices with listening capability must receive the next transmission and accept information on the data lines as either commands or addresses. When data is to be sent to addressed listeners, the ATN line is set high (not true).

2. IFC. This line is used only by the system controller to initialize the interface to a standby or idle state in which there is no activity on the bus. All devices must monitor this line at all times and respond to it within 100 microseconds. When IFC is set true, all devices addressed to either talk or listen are set to untalk or unlisten, and the serial poll function (if in use) is disabled.

3. REN. This line is used only by the system controller to place all listeners in the remote programming mode when they are addressed to listen. All devices capable of both local and remote operation must monitor the REN line and respond to it within 100 microseconds. When the system controller sets this line high (not true), all devices return to local operation.

4. SRQ. The Service Request line is used by one or more devices on the bus to indicate a need for attention, as might be caused by a syntax error, overload, etc. Such a request by any device can interrupt the current sequence of events. The SRQ line can be cleared by a serial poll only, and the controller must perform a poll of all devices on the bus to determine which one requires service.

5. EOI. When the ATN line is not true, the End or Identify line is used by an active talker to indicate the last byte of a data message. The IEEE-488 standard also permits the end of a transmission to be indicated by the generation of a line feed character (ASCII 10). When ATN is true, the controller uses this line to execute a parallel poll in which up to eight devices on the bus place a status bit on the eight data I/O lines.

UNIVERSAL COMMANDS

The five multiline universal commands are Device Clear, Local Lockout, Serial Poll Enable, Serial Poll Disable, and Parallel Poll Unconfigure. Unlike the four uniline commands already described (IFC, REN, ATN, IDY), these universal commands are transmitted on the data lines. Devices on the bus interpret such data as commands, since the ATN line is true. The universal commands are:

1. Device Clear (DCL). This command causes each recognizing device on the bus to return to a predefined state. The devices respond only if they are addressed or in remote control. The state at which each device is reset is defined by the manufacturer of the equipment.

2. Local Lockout (LLO). This command is used to disable the front panel controls or return to local pushbutton on those devices which recognize the command. This is useful during an automatic test sequence when it is mandatory that test personnel be prevented from altering a predetermined operating mode of the instrument or device.

3. Serial Poll Enable (SPE). This command causes all talkers on the bus to assume a serial poll mode. When each is addressed to talk the device will place on the bus data lines a single 8-bit word which contains information on the status of the device, as specified by the manufacturer of the equipment.

4. Serial Poll Disable (SPD). This command will follow the serial poll enable command so that each talker on the bus is returned to its normal state of outputting data when addressed to talk.

5. Parallel Poll Unconfigure (PPU). This command will reset all devices which recognize a parallel poll command so that they are in an idle state and unable to respond to it.

In addition to the five universal multiline commands described above, there are two additional universal commands which are technically classified as addresses. These are Untalk (UNT) and Unlisten (UNL).

The Untalk command unaddresses the current talker on the bus. It is not necessary to use this command to unaddress the current talker since addressing the next talker automatically unaddresses all others, but this command has been provided for convenience.

The Unlisten command unaddresses all listeners on the bus. It is not possible to unaddress one listener; all will be unaddressed. This command will precede addressing desired listeners when it is necessary that only such listeners receive the next data to be sent on the bus.

ADDRESSED COMMANDS

The following is a description of a group of commands which are called addressed commands. It is not necessary for devices on the bus to respond to any or all such commands, since the manufacturer of a GPIB instrument or device determines which, if any, are necessary for the proper operation of the unit when under remote control.

1. Group Execute Trigger (GET). This command causes all currently addressed devices which have GET capability to receive and respond to the command by initiating a preprogrammed action. For example. a voltmeter can take a reading, or a generator can produce a burst of oscillation. Some devices on the bus may also require an additional command to produce the desired function. The purpose of the GET command is to provide a trigger command which

can produce simultaneous triggering in all addressed devices.

2. Selected Device Clear (SDC). This command causes a currently addressed listener to reset to a predetermined state as specified by the manufacturer of the device.

3. Go to Local (GTL). This command causes the currently addressed listener to leave its remote state and return to manual front panel control. Should the device be read-dressed with a subsequent command, it will return to the remote mode.

4. Parallel Poll Configure (PPC). This command is used in conjunction with a secondary command, Parallel Poll Enable Command. It causes the addressed listener to be configured in accordance with the PPE command which follows it. When the device receives the PPC command from the controller, it responds on a particular data I/O line to indicate its status. Another secondary command, Parallel Poll Disable (PPD), prevents any response from the the addressed devices that have received the PPC command.

POLLING

The interface system provides two methods of interrogating listeners by the controller. These are referred to as parallel poll and serial poll. It provides the GPIB programmer with two methods of determining the status of the devices on the bus.

Serial polling is performed in the form of a sequence in which each device on the bus is individually addressed and directed to return a status byte to indicate its condition. The controller should be directed to poll every device on the bus to be sure that each SRQ requestor is found. When the serial poll is completed, the controller then must transmit the Serial Poll Disable and Untalk commands so that each device on the bus is returned to the normal remote state.

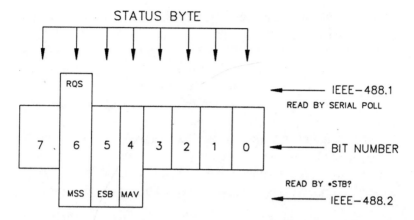

Figure 2-2.   Serial poll status byte as defined by IEEE-488.1 and IEEE-488.2.

The advantage of the serial pole sequence is that it will return to the controller the identity of the requestor at the same time as its status byte is received. However, when there are many devices on the bus (all devices should be polled), this can be a very time consuming procedure.

IEEE-488.1 originally provided the serial poll to allow controllers to read the status of the instruments on the bus, but other than bit 6, RSQ, it left the definition of the remaining bits to the manufacturer of the device. IEEE-488.2 further defines two more bits of the status byte (Figure 2-2).

Bit 4 is defined as the message available bit (MAV). This indicates whether or not the output queue of the instrument is empty. When data is available, bit 4 will be true.

Bit 5 is the event status bit (ESB), which is used to indicate if an enabled standard event has occurred. Such events include (but are not limited to) power on, user request, command errors, and execution errors.

A faster method of polling is the parallel poll, but only eight devices can be polled at a time and just 1 bit of information from each can be transmitted to the controller. If there are more than eight devices on the bus which must be polled, this may be done in two or more steps. When the parallel poll sequence is initiated by the controller, up to eight designated devices on the bus will return its status bit on one of the data I/O lines. Each device can be directed to respond on a particular data line through the direction of the secondary command, PPE, which follows the Parallel Poll Configure command. It is also possible for some devices to be hard wired so that they will always respond on a designated data line.

It is possible to have more than one device respond on a given data line since the open collector output circuits of the devices allow a parallel connection with a resulting AND or OR of the status bits.

MESSAGE TERMINATION

In the IEEE-488 interface system there is no stipulation as to how long a message may be, so there must be some method by which all devices on the bus can determine that a message is indeed terminated. There are three methods which may be employed to accomplish this task.

The device which is talking on the bus may add the printer formatting line feed character (ASCII 10) to the end of each message. Another method is through the use of the dedicated End or Identify line (EOI) contained in the interface bus itself. This line has two purposes, End or Identify, and the ATN line is used to distinguish between each. When ATN is false, the EOI line can be used by the active talker to indicate to the listener(s) that the last byte of a data message has occurred. The third method allows the EOI line to be asserted concurrently with the line feed character.

Since there is no guarantee that any particular listener on the bus will respond to all types of message terminations, some manufacturers of GPIB devices have designed into their units the capability of choosing the type of message termination that best services the

Table 2-2.   Typical Programmable Terminator Commands in a GPIB Device.

Command Syntax	Terminator
W0 (default)	Enable CR, LF, EOI
W1	Enable CR & LF only
W2	Enable CR & EOI only
W3	Enable CR only
W4	Enable LF & EOI only
W5	Enable LF only
W6	Enable EOI only
W7	Disable all output terminators

system. Table 2-2 is a representative illustration of the types of terminator commands which can be programmed into a Fluke digital meter. To implement any of these terminators, the meter would be instructed to do so when it is addressed by the controller.

It is possible to create certain errors in a GPIB program if care is not taken to ascertain that the message terminator selected by the software engineer is compatible with all units on the bus. In the case in which data is transferred by binary block communications, it is possible that a data byte could be configured as the ASCII line feed character 00001010. Should this occur in a system in which a listener is programmed to respond to LF, it will automatically terminate the message and dump any following data bytes.

Another problem may occur when a carriage return precedes the line feed character. A controller may end the transmission when it receives CR, leaving the unsent LF character in the talker. Then, when that device is instructed to talk again, it will send the leftover LF character as the first data byte, creating an error in the controller.

This possible source of confusion over the message terminators has been resolved with IEEE-P981 amendment, which does not permit GPIB instruments to generate carriage returns for any reason.

Chapter 3

The IEEE-488.2 Standard

OVERVIEW

The IEEE-488.2 revision was adopted 10 years after the GPIB had been in use and was designed to help eliminate many of the user problems which plagued the GPIB. Some of the problems encountered were:

1. Device interface capabilities which would vary from one manufacturer's unit to another, even though the type of instrument might be identical. For example, one digital voltmeter might be a listen-only device which could not report back to the controller its readings. Another might not be fully programmable — for example, it might require a manual setup of its function or range.
2. Data formats might be totally different from one unit to another. One might communicate in ASCII while another might require binary or BCD coding. It would be difficult to substitute such units for each other in a given test setup

without performing some time-consuming rewriting of software.

3. Message protocol was not standardized. The order in which a unit receives or transmits commands and data was strictly up to the designer of the instrument.

4. There was a wide variation in status reporting between units from each manufacturer. Since the function of most of the 8 bits of the status byte was left up to the discretion of the manufacturer, it would not be possible to replace one unit with another without first modifying the test programming.

5. Device-dependent commands were different even though two identical units performed the same function. The software engineer could not assume that any command, no matter how common or frequent it might be used, would be suitable for all similar type instruments.

These problems, and others, were solved for the most part by the adoption of the IEEE Standard 488.2 Codes, Formats, Protocols, and Common Commands for Use with ANSI/IEEE Standard 488.1 — 1987. Included in the new standard is a set of codes, data formats, message protocols, and common commands which would be used with, and in addition to, the original standard (now identified as IEEE-488.1). Figure 3-1 illlustrates the structure of the new standard as it enhances the original one.

INTERFACE CAPABILITIES

IEEE-488.2 defines a minimum set of capabilities which each instrument or device must implement. Table 3-1 is a tabulation of these required capabilities. A listing of code definitions of the interface capabilities tabulated are in Appendix D.

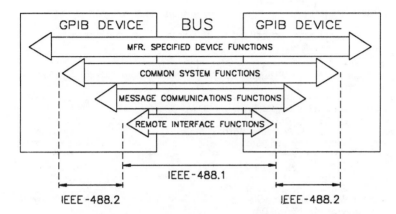

Figure 3-1   IEEE-488.1 and IEEE-488.2 functional structure.

SYNTAX AND DATA FORMATS

The IEEE-488.2 document specifies the required data format for any type of message that may be sent, including numbers and strings of characters. Included in the types of numbers which are specified are binary, octal, and hexadecimal. A listing of these

Table 3-1   Minimum IEEE-488.2 capabilities.

Capability	Code	Comment
Source Handshake	SH1	Full Capability
Acceptor Handshake	AH1	Full Capability
Talker	T(TE)5, or	Basic Talker, Serial
	T(TE)6	Poll, untalk on MLA
Listener	L(LE)3, or	Basic Listener,
	L(LE)4	Unlisten on MTA
Service Request	SR1	Full Capability
Device Clear	DC1	Full Capability
Remote Local	RL0 or RL1	None or Full Capability
Parallel Poll	PP0 or RL1	None or Full Capability
Device Trigger	DT0 or DT1	None or Full Capability
Controller	C0 or C4 with	None or Respond to SRQ,
	C5, C7, C8 or C11	Send IF Msg., pass,
		Receive control
Electrical Interface	E1 or E2	Open Collector or Tristate

Table 3-2   Required and optional data formats specified by IEEE-488.2.

LISTENER FORMATS	STATUS
<Decimal Numeric Program Data>	Required
<Character Program Data>	Optional
<Suffix Program Data>	Optional
<Non—Decimal Numeric Program Data>	Optional
<String Program Data>	Optional
<Arbitrary Block Program Data>	Optional
<Expression Program Data>	Optional
TALKER FORMATS	
<NR1 Numeric Response Data>	Required
<Arbitrary ASCII Response Data>	Required
<Character Response Data>	Optional
<NR2 Numeric Response Data>	Optional
<NR3 Numeric Response Data>	Optional
<Hexadecimal Numeric Response Data>	Optional
<Octal Numeric Response Data> Optional	
<Binary Numeric Response Data>	Optional
<String Response Data>	Optional
<Definite Length Arbitrary Block Response Data>	Optional
<Indefinite Length Arbitrary Block Response Data>	Optional

formats, some of which are optional for the equipment designer, is illustrated in Table 3-2.

In order to allow older GPIB devices to properly communicate with the newer instruments which are designed to comply with IEEE-488.2, a new concept has been introduced. This is referred to as precise talking and forgiving listening. This requires GPIB devices to accept a wide variety of data formats and codings so that the information transmitted on the bus is received and accepted without error (forgiving listening).

The exact opposite is true when the newer devices must talk on the bus (precise talking). The data transmitted by any IEEE- 488.2 instrument must adhere to a rigorous set of formats. This ensures that new devices will be able to communicate with those using the older formats such as IEEE 728. The concept of precise talking and forgiving listening is very important, and it ensures compatibility between older and newer GPIB devices.

DEVICE MESSAGE PROTOCOLS

Under the original IEEE-488 document, any device which received a message containing more than one command or data would be allowed to interpret and react to that transmission in any way that the manufacturer desired. This freedom of message protocol made it difficult for the software engineer to accurately predict how instruments or devices from various manufacturers would react to any given multiple message.

The IEEE-488.2 document carefully describes a message exchange protocol which is to be used on the IEEE-488.1 bus. In addition to specifying how multiple commands are to be received, it also describes what to do in the event that an incomplete command is sent or a device is interrupted during the processing time of a received message.

A set of device operational states has been defined to implement the device message protocol of IEEE-488.2. These states are tabulated in Table 3-3. Although there is very little chance for confusion when a device receives a single byte from the bus, it may become quite complicated when an incomplete or unterminated command is sent or the device is interrupted. IEEE-488.2 defines what the instrument or device must do under these circumstances.

Included in the device message protocol are specifications on the order in which data bytes are sent and how devices on the bus exchange data. A device cannot send data unless commanded to do so. If a new command is received, the output queue is cleared and that command is processed.

Table 3-3   Definitions of device operational states.

STATE	PURPOSE
IDLE	Wait for messages
READ	Read and execute messages
QUERY	Store responses to be sent
SEND	Send responses
RESPONSE	Complete sending response
DONE	Finished sending response
DEADLOCK	The device cannot buffer more data
UNTERMINATED	The device has attempted to read an unterminated message
INTERRUPTED	The device was interrupted by a new message while sending a response

COMMON COMMAND SET

Since most instruments and devices used in an ATE system use similar commands which perform identical functions, the IEEE-488.2 document has specified a common set of commands which all devices must use. This avoids the problem encountered with IEEE- 488.1 in which devices from various manufacturers used a different set of commands to enable functions and report status. The following set of command groups ensures that all devices communicate uniformly:

1. System data. These commands are used to store or retrieve information such as device identification, descriptions and options, protected user data, and resource description transfer. It is possible to determine the manufacturer and model of the device under remote control. Serial number and device options may also be reported, but this capability is not mandatory. Protected user data and resource description transfer are protected information which can be accessed by the controller only when the protection mechanism, such as a hidden switch, is disabled.

2. Internal operations. These commands include such instrument operations as resetting, self-calibrating, and self-test of a GPIB device. An optional command enables the controller to read the internal settings of the device. The self-calibration feature of the unit must not require any local user interaction and must not cause any conditions that would violate the IEEE-488.1 or 488.2 standards. The device may respond to a calibration query to indicate that the calibration was carried out successfully and report any calibration errors that may have occurred. The Reset command sets the device-dependent functions to a known state and must not affect the state of the IEEE- 488.1 interface, the Service Request Enable register, or Standard Event Status Enable register.

3. Status and event. These commands control the status structure of the GPIB device and provide a means to read and enable events. Included in these commands are Clear, Event Status Enable, Power-on Status, and Service Request Enable. The Clear Status command clears the status register and associated status data structures. The Power-on Status Clear command controls the automatic clearing of the Service Request Enable register, the Standard Event Status Enable register, and the Parallel Poll Enable register. With these registers cleared at power-on, the device is prevented from requesting service while the power-on-clear flag is true. The Service Request Enable command sets the Service Request Enable register which determines what bits in the Status byte will cause a Service Request from the device. The Status Byte Query command reads the status byte, causing the device to respond with an integer in the range of 0 to 255. The binary equivalent of the integer represents the contents of the status byte.

4. Synchronization. The operations of all devices within the system are synchronized with these commands. Included is

a Wait to Continue command which forces the device to complete all previous commands and queries. The Operation Complete command tells the device to set bit 0 in the Standard Event Status register when it completes all pending operations.

5. Parallel poll. The response to a parallel poll is controlled by these commands. It is also possible to obtain the same information from any device, without the need for an actual poll, by executing an Individual Status Query command. This permits the user to determine what an individual device would send on a parallel poll command.

6. Device trigger. These commands enable a device to be triggered and specify how it responds to the trigger message. The Define Device Trigger command stores a sequence of commands which the device will follow when the Group Execute Trigger (GET) is received. The Define Device Trigger query allows the user to review the command sequence which the device will follow upon receipt of the GET comand.

7. Controller. The control of the bus may be passed between devices using the Pass Control Back command. This command tells the potential controller what address to pass control back to. The command must be followed by a number, 0 to 30, which is the address of the device that is to become the next controller. It is also possible to pass control to a device which contains both a primary and secondary address. In this case the command is followed by two numbers.

8. Auto-configure. IEEE-488.2 defines an algorithm which permits the user to automatically assign talk and listen addresses to devices on the bus. Using this optional capability, it is possible to physically assemble a test system and allow the controller to query all devices to find out who they are, and then assign addresses. The Accept Address

command allows the controller to assign an address to each configurable device on the bus. As part of the automatic system configuration sequence, the Disable Listener Function command is used to cause a device to stop listening on the bus until it receives a Device Clear (DCL) command.

9. Macros. These optional commands enable the user to define new commands for the instrument under control. Macros can be used to provide shorthand for complex commands and reduce bus traffic. Other instruments can be emulated using these commands. The Define Macro command is used to assign a sequence of commands to a macro label. When the device receives the macro label as a command, it executes the sequence of commands contained within the macro. The macro label cannot be the same as a common command or query but may be the same as a device-dependent command. The Enable Macro command, followed by number 0, disables all macros so that a device dependent command which is the same as a macro can be executed. If the Enable Macro command is followed by a number in the range of -32767 to 32767, the macros will be enabled. The user can determine if macros are enabled on a device by sending the Enable Macro query. The Learn Macro query causes the device to respond with the labels of all defined macros, whether or not they are enabled. Macros may be purged from a device by using the Purge Macros command.

10. Stored Settings. These commands are used to save the state of the device under control, to be used at a later time. The Save command stores the present state of the device in the device's memory. If there is more than one location in which this data can be stored, the command is followed by a number which designates the storage register to use. The Recall command restores the state of the device, as stored in its memory from a previous Save command. As with the Save command, the Recall command must be followed by

a number to specify the register from which the stored settings are to be selected.

Note that all common commands are always sent in the data mode of the bus (ATN false). IEEE-488.2 specifies that certain common commands must be operational in a GPIB device, while others are left up to the discretion of the instrument designer. Table 3-4 illustrates the sets of the common commands, organized by command group. A description of the common commands is in Appendix E.

STATUS REPORTING

Status reporting defined by IEEE-488.2 builds upon and extends the original specifications of the status byte of the 488.1 document. Figure 3-2 illustrates the IEEE-488.2 status reporting model showing the IEEE-488.1 status byte, which can be read by either a serial poll or Status Byte Query. The 488.2 byte contains seven single-bit summary messages from Status Data Structures which are registers or queues. IEEE-488.1 defines the Recall Status Query (RSQ) bit, and IEEE-488.2 defines the event status bit (ESB) and message available bit (MAV). The user can enable a GPIB device to request service, depending upon the state of the summary bits of the status byte.

The status byte is transferred to the controller by means of the IEEE-488.1 serial poll or an IEEE-488.2-defined common query. Additionally, more common commands and queries are defined to obtain information from the devices under remote control. An overview of the IEEE-488.2 status reporting structure is shown in Figure 3-2.

The Status Byte register, illustrated in Figure 3-3, was originally defined by IEEE-488.1, which did not specify how the bits (other

Table 3-4   IEEE-488.2 comman commands, organized by command group.

MNEMONIC	DISCRIPTION	COMPLIANCE
	AUTO CONFIGURE COMMANDS	
• AAD	Assign Address	Opt.
• DLF	Disable Listener Function	Opt.
	SYSTEM DATA COMMANDS	
• IDN?	Identification Query	Reqd.
• OPT?	Option Identification Query	Opt.
• PUD	Protected User Data	Opt.
• PUD?	Protected User Data Query	Opt.
• RDT	Resource Description Transfer	Opt.
• RDT?	Resource Description Transfer Query	Opt.
	INTERNAL OPERATION COMMANDS	
• CAL	Calibration Query	Opt.
• LRN	Learn Device Setup Query	Opt.
• RST	Reset	Reqd.
• TST?	Self—Test Query	Reqd.
	SYNCHRONIZATION COMMANDS	
• OPC	Operation Complete	Reqd.
• OPC	Operation Complete Query	Reqd.
• WAI	Wait to Complete	Reqd.
	MACRO COMMANDS	
• DMC	Define Macro	Opt.
• EMC	Enable Macro	Opt.
• EMC?	Enable Macro Query	Opt.
• GMC?	Get Macro Contents Query	Opt.
• LMC?	Learn Macro Query	Opt.
• PMC	Purge Macros	Opt.
	PARALLEL POLL COMMANDS	
• IST?	Individual Status Query	Reqd. if PP1
• PRE	Parallel Poll Enable Register Enable	Reqd. if PP1
• PRE?	Parallel Poll Enable Reg Enable Query	Reqd. if PP1
	STATUS & EVENT COMMANDS	
• CLS	Clear Status	Reqd.
• ESE	Event Status Enable	Reqd.
• ESE?	Event Status Enable Query	Reqd.
• ESR?	Event Status Register Query	Reqd.
• PSC	Power on Status Clear	Opt.
• PSC?	Power on Status Clear Query	Opt.
• SRE	Service Request Enable	Reqd.
• SRE?	Service Request Enable Query	Reqd.
• STB?	Read Status Byte Query	Reqd.
	DEVICE TRIGGER COMMANDS	
• DDT	Define Device Trigger	Opt. if DT1
• DDT?	Define Device Trigger Query	Opt. if DT1
• TRG	Trigger	Reqd. if DT1
	CONTROLLER COMMANDS	
• PCB	Pass Control Back	Reqd. if Controller
	STORED SETTINGS COMMANDS	
• RCL	Recall Instrument State	Opt.
• SAV	Save Instrument State	Opt.

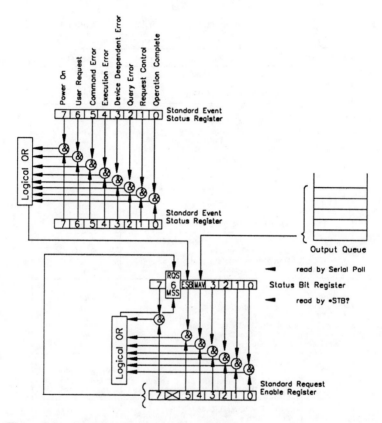

Figure 3-2   IEEE-488.2 status reporting model.

than RSQ) were to be set or cleared. This was left up to the discretion of the equipment manufacturer.

IEEE-488.2 defines additional commands which allow the user to access the status byte and associated data structures. Although a serial poll will clear the RSQ bit, it will not clear the status byte, which can be done by clearing the related status structures using the *CLS command.

The bits defined by IEEE-488.2 are bits 4, 5, and 6. Bit 4 is the message available bit (MAV) which is true if the output queue

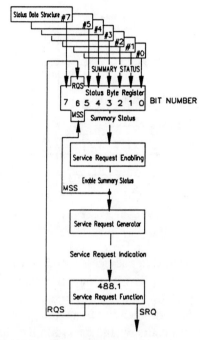

Figure 3-3   IEEE-488.2 status reporting structure.

contains data available to output. Bit 5, event status bit (ESB), indicates if an enabled standard event has occurred. The master summary status bit (MSS) is bit 6, which indicates if the device has at least one condition to request service. Note that the MSS bit is not considered part of the IEEE-488.1 status byte and will not be sent in response to a serial poll. The RSQ bit, however, if set, will be sent in a 488.1 serial poll.

Figure 3-4 illustrates the service request enabling operation. The user may set bits in the Service Request Enable register (SRER), corresponding to bits in the status byte. When a bit is set in the SRER, it enables that bit in the status register to request service.

Event registers are used to remember that a predefined condition changes in a device. IEEE-488.2 defines a command to read the Standard Event Status registor, but if a unit has more than one event

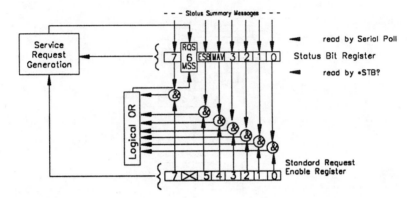

Figure 3-4   Service request enabling operation.

register, there must be other device-dependent commands to access the data stored within it. The bits, once set, cannot be cleared until done so by either reading the register or using the Clear command (*CLS). IEEE-488.2 defines the transition criteria which sets an event bit true. This occurs when its condition changes from either false to true or true to false.

A GPIB device may also provide Event Enable registers, which are similar to the Service Request Enable register. Setting bits in the Event Enable register permits bits in the Event register to be summarized in the status byte.

The Standard Event Status register (SESR) is a specific application of status reporting, and the IEEE-488.2 document specifies the meaning of each bit of the SESR. Figure 3-5 depicts the Standard Event Status register. The 8 bits of the SESR have been defined by IEEE-488.2 as specific conditions which can be monitored and reported back to the user upon request. These events are:

Bit 0, operation complete (OPC). This bit, generated in response to the OPC command, is set when the device has completed its current operations and is ready to accept a new command.

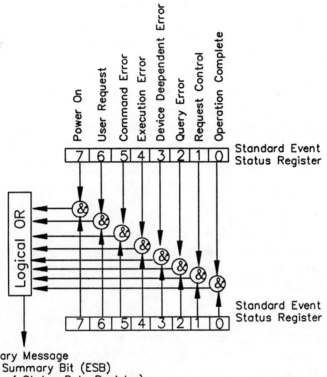

Figure 3-5   Standard event status register.

Bit 1, request control (RQC). This bit is used by a device to indicate to the controller that it wants to become the active controller on the bus.

Bit 2, query error (QYE). A query error, indicated by this bit, occurs when an attempt to read data from the output queue is made when no data is present or if some data was lost as in the event of a queue overflow.

Bit 3, device-dependent error (DDE). This bit is set when an error in a device function occurs, such as improper execution of a command due to an internal condition or malfunction of the device.

Bit 4, execution error (EXE). An execution error occurs when the command received by the device is not within its legal capability, or is not consistent with its designed operation. It may also occur when an internal condition prevents proper execution of a valid command.

Bit 5, command error (CME). This bit indicates that the device received a command that was a syntax error (not defined by 488.2 standard), a semantic error such as a misspelled command, or a command that the device does not implement. A group execute trigger (GET) received inside a program message will also cause a command error.

Bit 6, user request (URQ). This bit, set without regard to the remote or local state of a device, will be set when the user has activated a device defined control. Its purpose is to enable the user to obtain the controller's attention.

Bit 7, power on (PON). This bit indicates that the device's power source was turned off, then on, since the last time that the SSER was read.

All IEEE-488.2 devices have the Standard Event Status register and may also contain other event registers. The SESR is written with the Enable Status (*ESE) command and read with the Enable Status query (*ESE?). The register is automatically cleared when reading it via the ESE? query or sending the Clear command (CLS). The device designer has the option of clearing the register with the power-on transition and recording any transitions which occur subsequently.

Queues are used to allow a device to report to the controller status or other information in an orderly manner. Each queue has a summary message bit which is set when the queue contains information. The output queue of the IEEE-488.2 device uses the MAV bit in the status byte to indicate that it contains available data. This is a first-in, first-out (FIFO) queue, and it can be cleared only by a 488.1 Device Clear command, the Reset command, or by power on.

PARALLEL POLL

The parallel poll specified by the IEEE-488.1 document provided a means to quickly ascertain the status of each of the devices on the bus. IEEE-488.2 carries this capability further with an optional means of generating and controlling a device's response to a parallel poll. Figure 3-6 illustrates the structure of the 488.2 parallel poll data handling response. The structure of the parallel poll is the same as the Event register, but its summary bit is sent in response to a parallel poll and not in a status byte. This summary bit is referred to as IST, or individual status local message. An Enable register is provided to determine which events are summarized in the ist.

The Individual Status Query (*IST?) allows the user to determine the current state of the IST local message. This is the status that would be sent in response to a parallel poll. The query permits reading the response of the device without the need to perform an actual parallel poll.

The Parallel Poll Enable Register command (*PRE) sets the bits which determine what conditions are summarized in the IST. The command must be followed by a number which, when converted to binary, represents the bits set in the Parallel Poll Enable register.

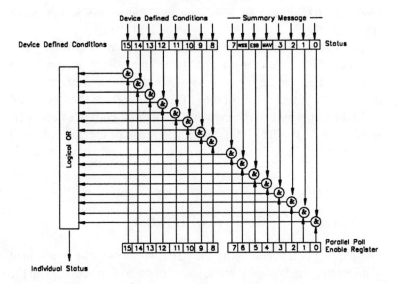

Figure 3-6   IEEE-488.2 parallel poll data handling response.

The Parallel Poll Enable Register Query (*PRE?) allows the device to respond with an integer in the range of 0 to 65535. This tells the user what bits are set in the PPER.

Chapter 4

GPIB Hardware

It is estimated that there are more than 4000 different instruments, produced all over the world, which are capable of remote control operation in an IEEE-488 interface system. It is beyond the scope of this book to describe them all. Subsequent chapters will provide information on hardware supplied by two of the major suppliers of such instruments, Hewlett-Packard and Tektronix. The following is a discussion of some of the types of GPIB hardware which is produced by these and several other manufacturers to enhance the operation of the interface system and make it more useful and easier to use.

PC TO GPIB INTERFACES

In the early days of the IEEE-488 interface system the number of manufacturers supplying controllers was very small, possibly being limited to just those which also designed and sold the slave instruments which were placed on the bus in automatic test systems. It soon became obvious, however, that the proliferation of the personal computer provided a very powerful tool with which to control the various talkers and listeners on the bus. Most personal computers could not speak the language or provide the necessary commands for the bus, and many manufacturers of computer ancillary equipment saw a need for IEEE-488 controller boards or plug-in boxes which could link the instruments on the bus to the computer. These are called PC interfaces. Today there are many manufacturers which can supply these interface boards and boxes which will allow almost any computer to speak the language of the IEEE-488 interface system. Through the use of the PC interface boards and plug-in boxes, it becames possible to select PC computers in favor of dedicated controllers to provide the commands on the bus.

There are two categories of PC interfaces: plug-in boards and external interface "black boxes." The former have proven to be far more popular not only for their higher speed but for the fact that external boxes are more cumbersome, usually attaching to the computer via the RS-232 interface connection or the Centronics compatible parallel port. A plug-in board results in a better, neater system. However, the external boxes operated via the RS-232 port of the computer are not restricted to the 20-meter limit placed on IEEE-488 instrumentation. An RS-232 link between computer and instrumentation allows as much as several hundred feet of separation.

IEEE-488 MODEMS

If it is necessary to locate the controller a very great distance from the rest of the interface system, it is possible to take advantage of a modem-to-IEEE-488 converter, which allows control of GPIB devices over virtually any distance if standard telephone lines exist at both locations. With such a system the serial interface limits the data transfer rate to several hundred kilobytes per second. If commands and data are sent relatively infrequently over the bus, this will not be a severe limitation.

Modem-to-IEEE-488 converters are available from several suppliers, one of which is IO Tech, 23400 Aurora Road, Cleveland, Ohio 44146. Their converter, MODEM488, provides standard Bell 103/212A type 110, 300, or 1200 baud modem signals to the IEEE-488 bus (Figure 4-1). Up to 14 GPIB devices may be connected to the converter, and it connects to the telephone line by means of a standard modular telephone connector. It operates in two modes: as a controller of IEEE-488 instrumentation (using commands and data received from a telephone line) and as a link between a controller and telephone line.

Modem-to-IEEE-488 converters may also incorporate additional features which can be very useful in a typical automatic test equipment (ATE) setup. For example, it is possible for the converter located at the remote location to automatically dial up the host controller in the event that any of the slave devices sends out a Service Request. The preprogrammed telephone number is stored in a nonvolatile memory, and the converter will automatically redial, if necessary, until the connection is made.

Modern modem-to-IEEE-488 converters are able to use simple, high-level commands, similar to those used by Hewlett-Packard controllers so that programming is no more difficult than what is already being provided to the host controller. The use of a modem allows ATE to be operated at remote locations without an operator present. This could prove to be a very valuable cost-saving system.

EXPANDERS AND EXTENDERS

Extending the maximum permissible distance between the controller and most distant device can also be implemented through the use of IEEE-488 bus extenders and expanders. An extender is a device which is placed between the host controller and the rest of

Figure 4-1   Modem to IEEE-488 interface. Courtesy of IO Tech.

the bus and is essentially transparent, or electrically invisible, to the system. Its function is to provide low-impedance driving power to the bus to handle the additional capacitance and inductance of bus cabling when more than the recommended 2-meter distance between devices is required. The function of an expander is slightly different; it is used when, in addition to the controller, more than 14 devices must be placed on the line. The functions of these two types of equipment are very similar, and manufacturers of such devices will often supply one unit to accomplish both tasks.

The use of an extender or expander is not limited to increasing the distance between devices or to enable more than 14 devices to be driven. For systems that are highly sensitive or need absolute isolation from power lines and other sources of interference, fiber optic data links are available. These are capable of extending the interface bus system as much as 1000 meters between controller and acceptors, while supplying very high electrical isolation and improved immunity from data transmission errors, which may be caused by any type of electrical interference. Fiber optic extenders are essentially transparent to the IEEE-488 interface system, but may require special techniques when performing certain operations. For example, speed requirements of the parallel poll function may preclude operation through a fiber optic link. To perform such an operation it is necessary for the controller to perform two polls. The data obtained from the first poll is discarded, and the second poll provides the desired report from the devices on the bus.

There are many manufacturers of expanders and extenders. One of these is the Hewlett-Packard Company, Palo Alto, California, which manufactures model HP 37204B multipoint HB-IB Extender (Figure 4-2). This device allows the normal 2-meter separation between GPIB devices to be extended to as much as 1250 meters, while allowing high-speed data rates. A fiber optic option is available. Multipoint capability means up to 30 remote sites can be daisy chained together, using only one 37204A extender at each site.

GPIB-to-RS-232 CONVERTERS

Since most computers manufactured today include the standard RS-232 port, it is not surprising that manufacturers of computer-to-IEEE-488 interfaces provide the necessary hardware to place these computers on the bus using that port. One such manufacturer is National Instruments, 12109 Technology Boulevard, Austin, Texas 78727 (Figure 4-3). Their RS-232-to-IEEE-488 interface, GPIB-232CV, consists of a stand-alone box which is microprocessor controlled and tailored for use as a RS-232-to-IEEE-488 converter. Its transparent conversion of data between the computer and GPIB bus requires no special commands or control codes, which makes it easy to implement into a system. Since data transfer between the

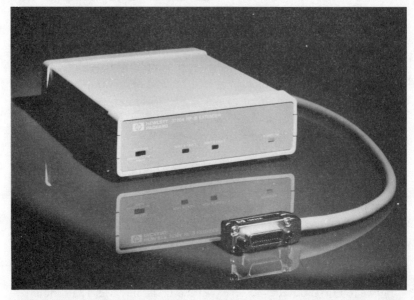

Figure 4-2   HP 37204A extender. Courtesy of Hewlett-Packard Co.

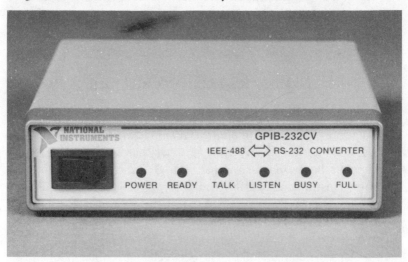

Figure 4-3   RS232 to IEEE-488 converter. Courtesy of National Instruments Inc.

bus and RS-232 port is bidirectional, this converter is also capable of converting any device which contains an RS-232 port into an IEEE-488 instrument.

As with many other types of IEEE-488 hardware, the National RS-232-to-IEEE-488 converter is not limited by the 20-meter restriction of maximum length between controller and interface devices, it allows relatively long cables to be used. Additional features include a built-in random access memory (RAM), of up to 256K bytes, to allow spooling of data during device operations.

PARALLEL IEEE-488 CONVERTER

A parallel IEEE-488 converter allows any unit which contains a Centronics parallel port to be used as a GPIB device. This type of converter is not as popular as the RS-232 device because a parallel port is output only, and it is generally used on listen-only devices such as printers or readouts. Manufacturers of parallel port converters have designed their product to be transparent (able to convert data in either direction) so that one such unit can be used either to connect a GPIB controller to a Centronics device or interface the Centronics port to the IEEE-488 bus. A buffer within the converter is able to store data while waiting for slower peripheral units to respond, thus freeing the host computer for the next operation. This type of converter is usually supplied as a stand-alone component which connects the IEEE-488 bus to the Centronics device with a pair of connectors.

ICS Electronics Corporation, 2185 Old Oakland Road, San Jose, California 95131, supplies model 4833 IEEE-488 parallel interface (Figure 4-4). This unit is a general-purpose, fully programmable unit which is available in both single- and dual-channel configurations. It is both a talker and listener in the GPIB system. As a talker it accepts parallel data (BCD or binary) and converts it to 8-bit characters for transmission on the bus. As a listener it receives data

Figure 4-4   IEEE-488 parallel data interface. Courtesy of ICS Electronics Corp.

from the bus and converts it to parallel words for use by a parallel input device.

DATA BUFFERS

Since the IEEE-488 interface system is designed with a handshake protocol, it is necessary for the communications on the bus to proceed at a rate which is determined by the slowest listener or talker on the line. This can lead to a very inefficient use of time, since faster devices on the bus will be waiting as the slower ones respond. Consider, for example, a slow printer. The host computer, and all devices on the bus, must wait until the printer has completed its task before the next communication can take place. Such a situation is readily improved through the use of an IEEE-488 data buffer, which increases the efficiency of the interface system by isolating a slow device.

An IEEE-488 data buffer has two ports. One is connected to the interface system and the other to the slow device which is to be isolated. The buffer receives the data on the first port, accepts it, and allows the bus to proceed with its normal operation. While this is happening, the received data is stored in memory as it is spooled to the device connected to the second port. Since the buffer is able to listen and talk on both ports, it is transparent to the bus. Through the use of a data buffer, it is commonly possible to improve the operating speed of a system by a factor of 10 or more.

IEEE-488-to-DIGITAL I/O INTERFACE

Many ATE systems have requirements which cannot be easily implemented by the use of stock components and must be custom designed to perform a dedicated task. One of the most useful categories of GPIB hardware which is commonly used in such situations is the IEEE-488-to-digital I/O interface, produced in several configurations by many suppliers. One such manufacturer is Seitz Technical Products, Inc., Avondale, PA 19311.

Seitz model 6450 IEEE-488-to-digital I/O interface consists of a stand-alone unit or a printed circuit board assembly which contains the standard GPIB interface connector (Figure 4-5). This component is both a talker and listener so that data can flow in both directions between the interface and the rest of the IEEE-488 system.

Although the interface hardware can send and receive data on the eight data I/O lines of the bus, its communications with the system is not limited to just 8 bits. Through the use of software commands, interface units are usually able to provide 40 or more data lines to the outside world which can be designated as input, output, or a combination of both. Other useful features can include additional functions on the data I/O lines, such as trigger output, status input, service request input, data latch input, clear, and inhibit.

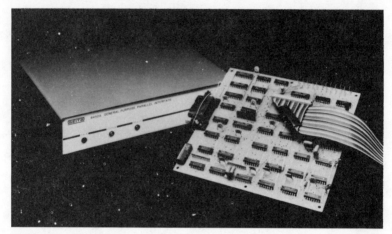

Figure 4-5   IEEE-488 to digital I/O interface. Courtesy of Seitz Technical
Products, Inc.

functions on the data I/O lines, such as trigger output, status input,
service request input, data latch input, clear, and inhibit.

A data I/O interface accessory allows the system designer to
custom design an ATE system. Through the use of software commands, any data generated by the system can be brought out to
peripheral devices and used in any way that is desired.

A standard Seitz digital interface allows 8 bits of data to be
received from the bus when in listener function, and can transmit
an 8-bit word when addressed to talk. The listen function provides
two output ports: standard TTL/Tri-state and a set of eight power
drivers. The power drivers consist of a set of open collector tran-
sistors which are rated at 30 volts and can sink up to 1 ampere of
current.

If more than 8 bits are required in the listen function, an optional
accessory (640 Option Module) is available. This accessory consists of a supplementary printed circuit board which contains a set
of eight registers, and is designed to be conveniently mounted to
the motherboard.

The Seitz 6450 digital IO interface accepts all 256 8-bit codes and does not recognize delimeter characters such as carriage return and line feed. For this reason these characters must be suppressed for proper data transfer unless they are desired. If not, they will appear on the output port as data.

Chapter 5

GPIB Devices and Functions

This chapter will describe some of the types of devices which are available with IEEE-488 implementation and will provide information on the various interface functions of which these instruments are capable. Since there are over 4000 instruments and devices produced with such capability, it is not possible to describe every type that is currently available. The best source of this information is from the manufacturers of GPIB devices; some of the major suppliers are covered in this chapter. Every manufacturer of electronic and electrical instrumentation knows that in order to be competitive in the marketplace the product line must be implemented for use in the GPIB system. Any instrument produced without such capability will probably have a counterpart, available from another source, which does. A search through the full-line catalogs of the manufacturers who produce the type of device of interest will usually result in finding an IEEE-488 instrument which will fill the desired requirements.

The following information represents only a very minute portion of the spectrum of IEEE-488 capable instruments, but it does show what can be obtained for a general automatic test system using the GPIB interface.

DIGITAL VOLTMETERS

Voltmeters represent one of the most basic test instruments, and it is not surprising that there is a vast selection from which to choose. A basic digital voltmeter with IEEE-488 capability can be obtained for substantially less than $1000 if a 4 1/2-digit instrument with limited GPIB capability will perform the required functions in the ATE system. A typical low cost instrument (about $674) is the Kiethley model 175/1753 autoranging DMM (Figure 5-1), which probably is one of the lowest cost GPIB digital voltmeters on the market. It can be operated in an ATE system as both a listener and a talker. The parameters of this meter which can be programmed under remote control are range, relative measurement, dB, EOI, trigger, SRQ, status, output format, and terminator. In addition it is possible to perform a calibration of the instrument under GPIB operation if the required reference and software are provided. It is not possible to select the meter function under remote control; this must be done manually.

A typical command to program the meter in HP-BASIC, assuming an address of 5, is:


```
OUTPUT 705 ; "F1R2T1X"
```


This will set the meter function, range, and trigger mode. The X at the end of the command is used as a command terminator. To set the meter to talk function so that the controller can store the meter reading, the command in HP-BASIC is:

Figure 5-1.   Keithley model 175 is a low cost DVM available with IEEE-488 compatibility. Courtesy of Keithley Instruments, Inc.

```
ENTER 705 ; V
```

The next available reading after this command has been received by the meter will be transmitted on the bus and stored in variable V in the controller memory, where it can be processed by further BASIC commands in the software.

The Keithly model 175/1753 is implemented for the following interface functions: SH1, AH1, T5, TE0, L4, LE0, SR1, RL2, PP0, DC1, DT1, C0, and E1. A full discussion of the various subsets of interface functions appears later in this chapter.

A full-function digital voltmeter (about $800) is the Fluke model 8840A (Figure 5-2), manufactured by John Fluke Mfg. Co. Inc., P.O. Box C9090, Everett, WA 98206. This is a first-class instrument which has a very respectable 0.005 percent dc accuracy

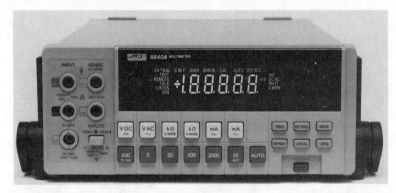

Figure 5-2.   High performance DVM for IEEE-488 systems. Courtesy of John Fluke Company.

specification and can equal or better the performance of other instruments which sell at higher prices. The 8840A is a 5 1/2-digit microprocessor controlled instrument which is available with IEEE-488 capability, and it can be calibrated while under remote control (using the proper voltage reference and software).

Under GPIB operation there is complete control of functions, ranges, and reading rates. This DVM supports the following IEEE-488 interface functions: SH1, AH1, T5, L4, SR1. RL1, DC1, DT1, E1, PP0, and C0. Its GPIB address is switch selectable by means of five switches at the rear panel. A sixth switch, when set to the ON position, forces the 8840 to assume a talk only mode in which it will ignore addressed commands from the bus and transmit readings that it measures in accordance with the front panel control settings.

A typical command string that might be sent from a Fluke 1722A controller is illustrated in Figure 5-3. The string configures the 8840A and triggers a reading. The PRINT command from the controller automatically sends terminators (CR, LF, and/or EOI) to the 8840A at the end of the command string.

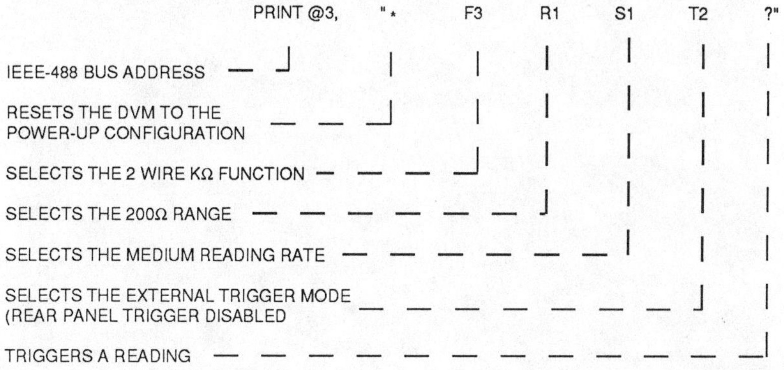

```
                    PRINT @3,    " *       F3      R1      S1      T2      ?"

IEEE-488 BUS ADDRESS  —  ⌐          |        |       |       |       |       |

RESETS THE DVM TO THE        _ _ ⌐          |       |       |       |       |
POWER-UP CONFIGURATION

SELECTS THE 2 WIRE KΩ FUNCTION — — — ⌐      |       |       |       |

SELECTS THE 200Ω RANGE  — — — — — — ⌐       |       |       |

SELECTS THE MEDIUM READING RATE — — — — — — |       |       |

SELECTS THE EXTERNAL TRIGGER MODE — — — — — — — — ⌐        |
(REAR PANEL TRIGGER DISABLED

TRIGGERS A READING  — — — — — — — — — — — ⌐
```

Figure 5-3.   Typical command string sent to the Fluke 8840A DVM from the 1722A controller.

OSCILLOSCOPES

It might seem at first glance that the presence of an oscilloscope in an automatic test system would require a technician to evaluate the display. This may be true under certain test setups, but modern GPIB oscilloscopes can talk back to the controller with a digitized message that contains waveform information. Using a graphics printer or plotter is all that is necessary to provide a hard copy of a waveform that can be analyzed at a later time. It would also be possible, using the graphics capability of the controller (if so equipped), to reproduce the waveform on the controller CRT or other display peripheral.

Although a top-of-the-line high-frequency digital oscilloscope does not come cheap, it is worth noting that the Tektronix model 2430 dual trace, 150 megahertz storage oscilloscope (Figure 5-4)

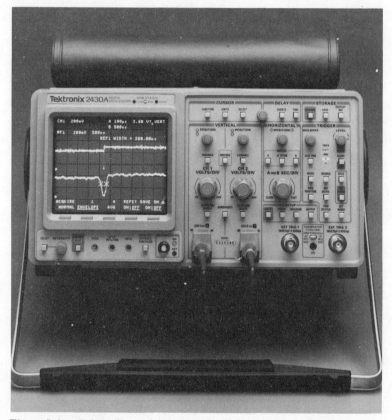

Figure 5-4.   Tektronix model 2430A digitizing oscilloscope. Courtesy of Tektronix, Inc.

is a state-of-the-art instrument which will provide sufficient capability for almost any ATE system.

GPIB programming capability is standard with full talk and listen modes. The instrument can transmit and receive waveform data at a transfer rate of 140 kilobytes per second. This oscilloscope is fully implemented for IEEE-488 interface functions SH1, AH1, T5, L3, SR1, RL1, DC1, DT0, PP0, and C0.

Figure 5-5.   Wavetek model 278 function generator. Courtesy of Wavetek, Inc.

SIGNAL GENERATORS

There is a vast array of signal generators available with GPIB capability. These include audio, pulse, RF, and function generators, as well as specialty products which are aimed at a specific portion of the ATE systems which require GPIB capability. One manufacturer of a wide selection of high quality IEEE-488-implemented signal generators is Wavetek, 9045 Balboa Avenue, San Diego, California 92123.

The Wavetek model 278 synthesized function generator (Figure 5-5) is a good example of a general-purpose instrument which can be used in a wide range of applications. This instrument can generate precise sine, triangle, and square waves over an 0.01 to 12 megahertz frequency range, and in synthesized mode the frequency accuracy is five parts per million (0.0005 percent). It can operate in continuous, triggered, gated, and burst modes with output levels to 29 volts peak-to-peak. Under GPIB control model 278 is implemented for interface subsets SH1, TE0, T6, RL1, AH1, L4, LE0, PP0, C0, SR1, DC1, and E2. Its GPIB address can be user selected by means of an internal set of switches or by the front panel GPIB address key. Verification of the address can be accomplished by pressing the ADR key on the front panel.

Wavetek model 278 will respond to an SRQ serial poll with a data byte which will indicate such problems as a blown fuse, program error, low battery level (for memory backup), and reference not locked to the external reference signal.

The 278 can be supplied with a memory retention battery so that up to 100 complete front panel settings can be stored. This permits power-up under GPIB control with any desired setting. Program commands to control the unit are straightforward and simple, usually consisting of a single letter followed by a number. For example, the command C0F1000 will direct the 278 to produce a sine wave of 1000 hertz. In this command C0 is used to set the generator to sine wave function and the letter F, followed by 1000, sets the frequency to 1 kilohertz. Once the unit is powered up under the desired default settings, it is necessary only to transmit on the bus each new setting as required.

UNIVERSAL COUNTERS

Unless there is a need for frequency measurement above the VHF range, a good choice for a frequency counter with IEEE-488 capability is the model 5334B (Figure 5-6) manufactured by the Hewlett-Packard Company, 3155 Porter Drive, Palo Alto, CA 94304. This is a general-purpose counter which has a range of 100 megahertz. It provides a nine-digit display and includes the usual functions of a universal counter such as period measurement and

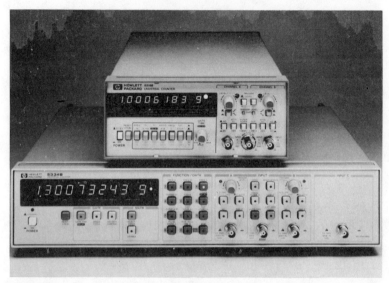

Figure 5-6. Two high-performance frequency counters available from Hewlett-Packard Co. Courtesy of Hewlett-Packard Co.

ratio A/B. The GPIB interface functions which this instrument supports are SH1, T3, TE0, L4, LE0, SR1, RL1, PP0, DC1, C0, and E2.

PROGRAMMABLE DC POWER SUPPLIES

All automatic test systems require a source of power (ac or dc) to operate the unit under test, and many times it is necessary to vary the input voltage to a unit to determine how it will function under low and high line voltage levels. In addition to this it may be desirable to check the response of a unit when it is subjected to voltage spikes and surges. These types of tests are readily attainable through the use of GPIB controlled programmable power supplies. A check through the full line catalog of any of the many power

Figure 5-7.   Typical programmable dc power supply. Courtesy of Lambda Electronics.

supply manufacturers will reveal what remote programmable units are available.

One such manufacturer of GPIB controllable dc power supplies is Lambda Electronics, 515 Broad Hollow Road, Melville, NY 11747. Their IEEE-488 programmable power system is a modular design which provides the communication link between the controller and up to six separate power supplies (Figure 5-7). Both output voltage and current limit can be programmed using one primary GBIB address and six secondary addresses. An additional feature, called Confidence Check, enables the GPIB system to perform an actual measurement of the output voltage or current limit of up to five power supplies. (The installation of the Confidence Check feature uses up one interface card slot in the Lambda power system and requires the use of a customer supplied GPIB controlled digital voltmeter).

Accuracy and resolution of the programmed output voltage of the power supplies is equal to 0.1 percent of full-scale, and the current limit can be set to within 2 percent of the programmed value plus 1 percent of full scale.

The Lambda IEEE-488 system is capable of a listen-only function. Confidence Check is accomplished through the use of an external GPIB voltmeter which is switched to any one of five power supplies by means of relays located on the Confidence Check card.

To program the output voltage of the Lambda programmable power supply, it is necessary to specify the primary address, which is user selectable by means of a 5-bit switch located on the rear panel, and the secondary address (1 to 6), which is hard wired into the unit. The voltage level is programmed by a command which consists of the letter P followed by four numbers which represent the percentage of full-scale voltage output in four significant digits.

Programming the desired current limit the next two values of the command consists of two numbers which represent the percentage of full scale current in two significant digits. The letter E must terminate all programming commands since it is the command string delimiter.

Assuming a primary address of 6 and a secondary address of 2, a typical command from a Fluke 1722A controller might be

```
PRINT @ 6:2, "P750050E"
```

This will program the Lambda power supply to deliver 75 percent of its full-scale output voltage with a current limit of 50 percent of maximum.

Confidence Check programming instructs the relays in the power supply to connect the desired output to the externally supplied voltmeter. The command for this check in the unit of the above example (assuming the Confidence Check card was inserted at location 1 secondary address) would be

```
PRINT @ 6:1, "CV2E"
```

This will provide monitoring capability of the output voltage of the power supply at location 2. To monitor current instead of voltage, the letter V in the command would be substituted by an I. Note that additional software commands are required to instruct the digital meter to report its reading to the controller to verify that the power supply has indeed responded properly to its command.

PROGRAMMABLE AC POWER SUPPLIES

Since many products which are tested with an ATE system are powered by an ac power source, GPIB controlled ac power is often used to provide a thorough test of such products under conditions of low line, high line, frequency variations, and power surges and transients.

To simulate such actual line voltage conditions for a unit under test, there are available ac power supplies which are capable of being programmed via the GPIB bus in an ATE setup. One supplier of such products is Behlman Engineering, 1142 Mark Avenue, Carpinteria, CA 93013. Their series of programmable ac power sources named Fiskars (Figure 5-8) is available in power ratings from 100 VA to 54 kVA, one, two, and three phase. Such parameters as output voltage, frequency, phase-to-phase angle (on multiphase units), and current limit can be programmed and controlled on the IEEE-488 bus. Fiskars programmable ac power sources are implemented in the following interface subsets: AH1, SH1, T6, TE0, L4, LE0, SR1, RL1, PP0, DC0, DT0, and C0.

Figure 5-8.   Picture of Behlman power supply. Courtesy of Behlman Engineering Co,

RELAY SWITCHERS

One of the most versatile GPIB devices which can be used to perform a range of functions is the relay switcher, such as manufactured by ICS Electronics Corporation, 2185 Old Oakland Road, San Jose, California 95131. Their model 4874B Relay Output Interface (Figure 5-9) provides up to 24-SPST low- or high-level relay contacts which can be controlled by software commands on the IEEE-488 bus. Relay contacts can be controlled individually or in a complete set. The test engineer can use a unit such as this to provide interconnections as required between various instruments and devices in an ATE system, all under GPIB control.

Programming commands to open or close any or all of the relays can be accomplished in one command string. The command for any given relay is the letter R, followed by the relay number, and then the digit 1 for close or 0 for open. A typical command, using HP-BASIC, is:

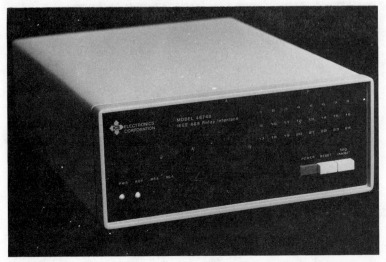

Figure 5-9.   ICS model 4874B relay switcher. Courtesy of ICS Electronics
Corp.

```
OUTPUT 704 ; "R140R151"
```

This command, assuming the 4874B has an address of 4, forces
relay 14 to open and relay 15 to close. Since the relay switcher
contains 24 relays, it is possible that some commands can be very
cumbersome if many relays need to be controlled. One way to solve
this problem when a given set of relays must be commanded to a
certain configuration many times in a program is to assign to a string
variable, such as R$, the complete instruction set. In this way the
software need only contain the statement OUTPUT 704 ; R$ to
accomplish the same task.

An additional feature of this device is the capability to provide
BCD interface on the bus. It will accept parallel data on 24 lines, 1
bit per line, and, as a talker, it can transmit this data on the GPIB
interface system. This permits up to six digits of information to be
sent on the bus from any source supplying BCD data or any other

type of data on 24 lines. Model 4874B is implemented for interface functions SH1, AH1, TE5, LE3, SR1, PP1, RL0, DC1, DT1, E1, and C0.

INTERFACE FUNCTIONS AND SUBSETS

Most manufacturers of instruments and devices which are GPIB controllable list the various interface functions which are implemented in the product. These capabilities can usually be found in the data sheets for the product, and in some cases they are marked on the instrument itself (usually near the GPIB connector). Although there are just 11 basic interface functions, the various subsets of these functions number much more than this. Table 5-1 illustrates the various subsets of each of the basic interface functions.

In Table 5-1 under the talker and listener functions, extended talker and extended listener refer to those devices which are capable of accepting secondary address commands. Additionally, MTA and MLA are the mnemonic for "my talk address" and "my listen address." When an addressed device receives the command to talk or listen, the command is referred to as MTA or MLA.

Although only six subsets of the controller function are listed, it should be noted that the IEEE-488 document specifies a total of 29 controller subsets. Those tabulated in Table 5-1 are the most significant levels.

When selecting instruments and devices to be used in a GPIB system, it is important to note the interface function subsets of which any product of interest is capable. These are specified by the manufacturer of the device who has determined what functions (and at what level) are required for the product to perform its desired capabilities. It is entirely possible that one or more desired interface functions are completely absent in a unit under consideration. Should this occur, it will be necessary to seek out a different product

Table 5-1.   Table of interface functions and subsets.

Interface Function	Basic Code	Capability Code
Source Handshake	SH	SH0 — No capability
		SH1 — Full capability
Acceptor Handshake	AH	AH0 — No capability
		AH1 — Full capability
Talker (extended talker)	T(TE)	T(TE)0 — No capability
		T(TE)1 — Basic talker, serial poll, talk only
		T(TE)2 — Basic talker, serial poll
		T(TE)3 — Basic talker, talk only
		T(TE)4 — Basic talker
		T(TE)5 — Basic talker, serial poll, talk only, unaddresses if MLA
		T(TE)6 — Basic talker, serial poll, unaddresses if MLA
		T(TE)7 — Basic talker, talk only, unaddresses if MLA
		T(TE)8 — Basic talker, unaddresses if MLA
Listener (extended listener)	L(LE)	L(LE)0 — No capability
		L(LE)1 — Basic listener, listen only
		L(LE)2 — Basic listener
		L(LE)3 — Basic listener, Listen only, unaddresses if MTA
		L(LE)4 — Basic listener, unaddresses if MTA
Service Request	SR	SR0 — No capability
		SR1 — Full capability
Remote/Local	RL	RL0 — No capability
		RL1 — Full capability
		RL2 — No local lockout
Parallel poll	PP	PP0 — No capability
		PP1 — Remote configuration
		PP2 — Local configuration
Device clear	DC	DC0 — No capability
		DC1 — Full capability
		DC2 — Omitselective device clear
Device trigger	DT	DT0 — No capability
		DT1 — Full capability
Driver electronics	E	E1 — Open collector, 250 Kilobytes/sec max
		E2 — Tri-state, 1 Megabyte/sec max

Table 5-1.   *(continued)*

Interface Function	Basic Code	Capability Code
Controller	C	C0 — No capability C1 — System controller C2 — Send IFC and take charge C3 — Send REN C4 — Respond to service request C5 — Send interface messages, receive, control pass control to self, parallel poll, take control synchronously

or work around the deficiency through the use of programming techniques (if possible).

One should be aware that it is possible that one instrument in a GPIB system may not be compatible with others if they each do not share the same desired interface function. For example, if it is necessary for local control of all instruments in a system to be locked out to prevent tampering by personnel, but the power supply feeding the unit under test does not have the local lockout function, the test engineer would not be able to implement this feature to cover all instruments in the ATE system.

PROGRAMMING REQUIREMENTS

When a GPIB interface system is fully assembled, complete with controller, it is virtually useless until the program or software is written and loaded into the controller's memory. The program will contain the instructions which will cause each and every device on the bus to perform the desired task.

Table 5-2.   Command Configuration.

Hewlett Packard 85B (BASIC)	OUTPUT 701;"F1R3"
Hewlett Packard 9825 (HPL)	wrt 701;"F1R3"
Fluke 1722A BASIC	PRINT @ 1%,"F1R3"
Tektronix 4050 BASIC	PRINT @ 1: "F1R3"
Tektronix 4041 BASIC (high level)	PRINT #1: "F1R3"
Tektronix 4041 BASIC (low level)	Wbyte atn(unt,unl,mta,1),"F1R3"

In order to properly write the program, the test engineer must be familiar with two major programming categories: the language the controller "speaks," and the correct syntax for each and every instrument or device under control.

Because of the large selection of controllers and slave instruments which are available for GPIB use, there is also a wide range of software commands that must be implemented to produce the desired performance in an ATE system. Unfortunately each different manufacturer has developed its own GPIB language, and more often than not there is no correlation between the products from one company to another. A message to a device under IEEE-488 control is composed of at least three parts: the output command from the controller, the address of the intended recipient, and the message itself. Table 5-2 illustrates how the identical command, F1R3, must be sent by six different controllers.

In general, a software program for automatic test equipment using the GPIB interface system may be written as a series of commands which follow a logical sequence in accordance with the requirements of the test. For example, if an audio amplifier is the unit under test, the ATE system might be composed of an audio signal generator, distortion analyzer, digital voltmeter, oscilloscope, and relay switcher controlling several different load resistances.

Instructions for performing the test are presented on the controller monitor so that the test technician is prompted in the proper connection of all parts of the test setup. When the test is started by a manual entry into the controller keyboard by the technician, the system is initialized by commands from the controller. Such things as setting the instrument controls to the proper setting and applying the desired load resistance to the output of the amplifier are automatically accomplished.

At this point the test would begin as the signal generator was set to each of several different frequencies and amplitudes. For each of these inputs to the amplifier under test the distortion analyzer would be instructed to take a distortion reading and then transmit that information to the controller for storage. For each frequency setting the oscilloscope could be instructed to send waveform data back to the controller for reproduction at a later time. This entire sequence could then be repeated for other values of load resistance as the relay switcher was instructed to connect new values to the output of the amplifier.

When the test was completed, the results could then be printed on a test data sheet, even including the output waveform as part of the hard copy of the test. Test specifications such as allowable limits of distortion and frequency response could be included in the software so that a Pass or Fail flag would be imprinted in the hard copy of the test data sheet.

The entire test sequence, briefly described above, is simply a series of commands which the controller would send to the various instruments of the system. It is up to the test engineer to write the program in the proper sequence and then debug it so that the final result is the exact test which is required for the unit under test.

When writing the program for any test sequence, the programmer must be familiar with the proper syntax not only for the controller but for each instrument and device on the bus as well. If a particular test involves many different types of devices, it could be quite time consuming to write and debug a program. Because all commands on the bus not only must be made in the proper sequence but must be absolutely correct in syntax, one may find that writing a software program for the IEEE-488 interface system is not as easy as it sounds.

This problem has been all but eliminated by several companies which have developed specialized software programs for the IEEE-488 bus. One such source of this material is Wavetek, in a product called Wavetest which provides syntax free programming for a wide selection of selected GPIB instruments.

Wavetest is a new generation of GPIB software which allows a PC/AT computer to be used as a powerful controller on the IEEE-488 bus. It contains an instrument library of over 50 general purpose instruments manufactured by such companies as Hewlett-Packard, Tektronix, John Fluke Company, and others, and it simulates the actual front panel of each instrument on an interactive "soft panel."

Each library contains the look-up table of a particular instrument's GPIB syntax and commands, together with the corresponding English language descriptions. In this way it is not necessary that the test engineer write the required commands in the format specified by the instrument manufacturer. All that is necessary is to literally tell the controller what kind of test should be run, what instruments to use, and what to do with the data. Wavetest does the rest by writing the program codes and GPIB commands for the entire set of instruments in the test setup.

COMMUNICATIONS FORMAT

Although the IEEE-488 document does not mandate any particular language or commands when sending data to the active listeners on the bus, device dependent commands sent from the active talker to the addressed listeners have been somewhat standardized through the experience of companies such as Hewlett-Packard in the design of GPIB instruments. This has resulted in a generalized code of format structure when the bus is in the DATA mode (ATN false).

The format for programming data strings consists of a set of alphanumeric characters as illustrated in Table 5-2. In this format system one or more alpha characters identifies a particular parameter, and a numeric sequence immediately following sets the numeric value. It is possible to set every parameter to the desired values by means of transmitting one string. Each device on the bus, however, will have its own unique string to define the required operation mode or status of the instrument.

In Table 5-2 the string "F1R3" is a typical command which contains sufficient information to set a digital voltmeter to the desired function and range. Note that it usually is not necessary to specify every parameter of which an instrument is capable. Most manufacturers of GPIB instruments include a default feature which automatically sets the device to a standard form of operation when any particular parameter is not specifically called out in the software commands. The default condition of any parameter is usually selected by the manufacturer of the instrument or device and is a commonly used setting or mode which is enabled at power-up of the instrument.

The original IEEE-488 document did not include guidelines for preferred syntax and format but through continued work in this area a new document, IEEE-728-1982, was created. This is entitled, "Recommended Practice for Code and Format Conventions for IEEE Standard 488." It contains guidelines (and not absolute standards) to increase the usability of equipment from different vendors. Through the use of standard syntax and formats the role of the software engineer is greatly eased. A similar document, IEC 625-2, contains similar information to IEEE-728 but it is not identical. A graphical depiction of the new documentation is illustrated in Figure 5-10.

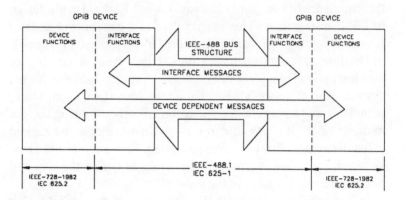

Figure 5-10.   IEC 625-2 depiction.

The original IEEE-488 document (now called IEEE-488.1 did not specifically define a data format or coding protocol. It simply stated that binary, BCD, or any standard alphanumeric code may be used. This allowed the designers of early GPIB systems to arbitrarily select any type of format which was convenient for them to use. During the early years the GPIB system solved many problems, but also created others when the format used by one manufacturer of automatic test equipment was entirely different from that of another. It soon became apparent that some type of communications format had to be specified. This problem was taken care of with the introduction of the IEEE-488.2 document, which defined a set of data codes and formats for everything from decimal numbers to arbitrary strings of characters.

Although IEEE-488.1 used the ASCII 7-bit code to document the interface commands, some GPIB devices used different forms of binary coding for information exchange. This deficiency was corrected in IEEE-488.2, which specifies three sets of codes: ASCII 7 bit for alphanumerics, binary 8-bit integer code, and binary floating point. A description of the floating point format appears in Appendix F.

By using the three codes specified in the IEEE-488.2 document, it is possible to define data formats for decimal, octal, and hexadecimal integers. Additionally, decimal floating point numbers, strings, character strings, and arbitrary strings can be defined.

Chapter 6

Programming the IEEE-488 GPIB

OVERVIEW

The IEEE-488 interface system has been widely accepted throughout the world, and there is a wide selection of controllers (including personal computers), hardware, and software packages which have been designed to make the GPIB system easier to implement and more useful. Before attempting to use a simplified system of so-called friendly software, the test engineer should have a fair command of at least one language with which he or she can create a dedicated test program using the GPIB instruments and devices at hand. It is important to understand the concept of the IEEE-488 programming system. Using a canned software program to avoid the hard work and long hours of designing and debugging a custom test setup may seem enticing, but it will not allow the engineer to understand the intricacies of the well-designed IEEE-488 system.

GPIB programs are written in controller language, and manufacturers of controllers such as Hewlett-Packard, Tektronix, and Fluke have developed languages which are not interchangeable with each other. It is the purpose of this chapter to provide some insight into these languages which are used in GPIB programming. When one such language has been mastered, the others will be understood as well, since there is not a great dissimilarity of the GPIB syntax of each of the languages.

HEWLETT-PACKARD BASIC

BASIC is very readable and friendly and is relatively easy to learn. Hewlett-Packard controllers such as the HP 85, HP 9845, and HP 9000 family of controllers use a variation of this language called HP-BASIC. The commands which are used to communicate with the slave instruments on the bus are not very complicated, and the syntax has been selected to be easy to read and very friendly. Table 6-1 is a listing of the most commonly used controller commands in the HP-BASIC language. In this table the controller is assumed to have a select code of 7 (the Hewlett-Packard convention for a GPIB controller), and the addressed listener and/or talker an address of 03.

HPL (HEWLETT-PACKARD LANGUAGE)

HPL preceded HP-BASIC and, as such, is not as elegant. It is, however, very similar in function even though the syntax is quite different. The program is written in lowercase lettering, and there is much abbreviation compared to BASIC. Table 6-2 illustrates the

Table 6-1.   Illustration of controller commands written in HP-BASIC.

Command	Function
Clear 7	Used to initialize the port.
Output 703	Talk command for the controller; used to send messages to the addressed listener.
Enter 703	Talk command for addressed talker; controller receives the outputted data.
Send 7 ; UNL	Universal unlisten command causes all units to unlisten.
Trigger 703	Triggers addressed listener to perform a function.
Local 703	Forces addressed listener into local operation.
Remote 703	Forces addressed listener into remote operation.
Clear 703	Clears addressed listener to default functions.

GPIB commands which are used to address and control the bus. As in the HP-BASIC command tabulated above, the Hewlett-Packard convention is to have the controller select code, 7, precede the primary listener/talker address.

Table 6-2.   Controller commands written in HPL language.

Command	Function
cli 7	Initializes the port
wrt 703	Talk command for the controller; used to send messages to the addressed listener
red 703	Talk command for addressed talker; controller receives the outputted data
trig 703	Causes addressed listener to perform a function
lcl 703	Forces the addressed listener into local operation
rem 703	Forces addressed listener into remote operation
clr 703	Clears addressed listener into default functions

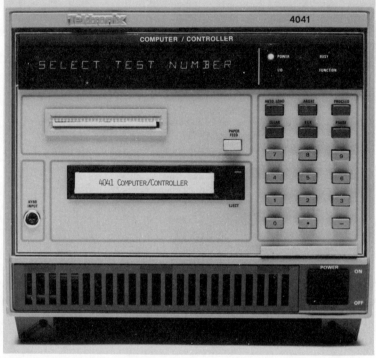

Figure 6-1.   Picture of Tektronix 4041

4041 BASIC (TEKTRONIX)

Textronix manufactures a GPIB controller (Figure 6-1) model 4041, which is implemented with the easy-to-use Extended BASIC language. The high-level commands of which this controller is capable allow the user to control the GPIB without the need to understand the IEEE-488 protocol. The controller automatically takes care of the handshake, bus transfers, etc.

The 4041 BASIC language is easy to use and powerful, and it is capable of both high-level and low-level GPIB commands.

English-like syntax provides a friendly programming language. To improve self-documentation the 4041 features the following:

- Variable names of up to eight characters
- FORTRAN-like subprogram calls
- Variable passing from main programs to subprograms
- Local and global variables
- 512K of directly addressed memory

As with all Tektronix GPIB products, the 4041 adheres to the codes and formats standard.

FLUKE 1722A CONTROLLER

The Fluke model 1722A (Figure 6-2) is an instrument controller which has been designed to be used with a touch-sensitive CRT display as the primary interface between itself and an operator. Its keyboard is used as the programming medium and may be unplugged and removed during operation as an instrumentation controller. Operating software is contained on either a floppy disk or nonvolatile RAM, and IEEE-488 operation is fully supported.

The touch-sensitive CRT display is friendly and well-suited for applications in which semiskilled personnel are required to operate highly complex, sophisticated equipment. No keyboard is required, and the CRT screen prompts the operator one step at a time.

The 1722A GPIB interface can transfer commands and data at a rate of 30 kilobytes per second. When operating as an IEEE-488 controller, this unit may be programmed in BASIC, compiled BASIC, or Extended BASIC as determined by the software package which is used.

Compiled BASIC provides greater flexibility and speed (3 to 5 times faster) than Fluke interpreted BASIC, and it includes the capability of linking subroutines in FORTRAN or assembly lan-

Figure 6-2.   Picture of Fluke 1722A

guage. Long descriptive variable names as well as large multiple-line statements are possible. Labels may be used in place of line numbers for branch targets, but the use of line numbers remains an option with the programmer. This freedom of format results in readable, structured BASIC programs.

The Extended BASIC option provides a compiler that allows the programmer to easily develop large (up to 2 megabytes) BASIC programs. The features of this option include all those provided by compiled BASIC, but the speed of execution is twice as fast as

Table 6-3.   Comparison between the three programming language options of the Fluke 1722A Instrument Controller.

Feature	Interpreted BASIC	Compiled BASIC	Extended BASIC
Program size	28K	35K	2M
Relative speed	1	3 to 5	2
Immediate mode commands	Yes	No	No
3-D arrays	No	Yes	Yes
long variable names	No	Yes	Yes
True subroutines	No	Yes	Yes
Program libraries	No	Yes	Yes
Input line statement capacity	80	510	510
Global variables	No	No	Yes
Step mode debugging	Yes	No	No

Fluke interpreted BASIC. Table 6-3 illustrates the features which each of the three Fluke BASIC languages offer.

PROGRAMMING SYNTAX OF THE 1722A

The programming syntax for the Fluke 1722A controller is very much similar to that of the Tektronix system. This is illustrated in Table 6-4, in which the most widely used commands to send and receive messages and data on the bus are shown. In the examples in Table 6-4 the addressed device is assumed to have a GPIB address of 3, and port 0 of the Fluke controller is in operation. As with all other high-level controllers, the Fluke 1722A has a command of the BASIC programming language which permits the software engineer to integrate the GPIB commands into a program which will perform the automatic test sequence as desired.

Table 6-4.   Programming syntax of the Fluke 1722A controller.

Command	Function
INIT PORT 0	Places the bus in an idle state, sending REN, IFC, UNL, UNT, and PPU messages.
CLEAR @3	Clears addressed device to default functions.
REMOTE @3	Sets REN line true and forces addressed device into remote operation.
LOCAL @3	Forces addressed device into a local state so that front panel controls become active.
PRINT @3	Talk command for controller to send message to addressed listener.
INPUT @3	Talk command for addressed listener to send data back to controller.
TRIGGER @3	Instructs addressed device to perform a function.
IF SPL(3%) THEN ...	Performs a serial poll on addressed device and proceeds to SRQ routine.
Y% = PPL(0%)	Assigns the results of a parallel poll on port 0 to integer variable Y.

PROGRAM COMPARISONS BETWEEN HP, TEKTRONIX, AND FLUKE

One can see that there is not a great dissimilarity between the GPIB syntax of the three BASIC languages required by the controllers manufactured by Hewlett-Packard, Tektronix, and Fluke Companies. The best way to compare one language with another is to illustrate a simple GPIB program, written in each of the languages, which will perform with a typical set of GPIB instruments. In the following examples a Wavetek model 278 function generator, driving an amplifier under test, will be commanded to assume a desired output setting, and a Fluke model 8430 voltmeter will be instructed to report back to the controller the output voltage of the amplifier as measured by the voltmeter.

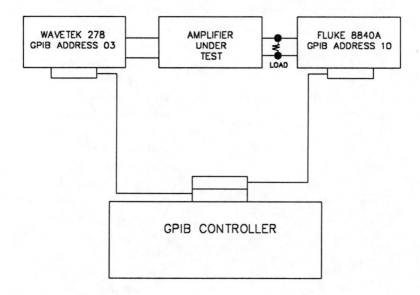

Figure 6-3.   Amplifier test setup.

The test setup is illustrated in Figure 6-3, and the addresses of the signal generator and digital voltmeter are assumed to be 03 and 10, respectively. Each of the following program examples are identical in function, line for line.

HP-BASIC Program

```
100 CLEAR 703, 710              Sets GPIB instruments
                                to default functions
110 OUTPUT 703 ; "F1000C0A0.1P1"  Sets function generator
                                to 1000 hertz, sine
                                wave, 0.1 volts peak-
                                to-peak, output on
```

```
120 OUTPUT 710 ; "F2R3S1T0"
```
Sets digital voltmeter to power-up configuration, ac function, 20-volt range, medium reading rate, continuous trigger

```
130 ENTER 710 ; V
```
Instructs voltmeter to report back to the controller its voltage measurement and place it into variable V

```
140 W = 2.83 * V
```
Calculates the peak-to-peak value of V and places it into variable W

```
150 G = W/0.1
```
Calculates amplifier gain (output/input)

```
160 DISPLAY G
```
Displays gain on controller CRT

```
170 END
```

FLUKE 1722A BASIC Program

```
100 CLEAR
110 PRINT @ 3, "F1000C0A0.1P1"
120 PRINT @ 10, "F2R3S1T0"
130 INPUT @ 10, V
140 W = 2.83 * V
150 G = W/.1
160 PRINT G
170 END
```

TEKTRONIX 4041 BASIC Program

```
100 INIT
110 PRINT #3  :  "F1000C0A0.1P1"
120 PRINT #10:  "F2R3S1T0"
130 INPUT #10  :  V
140 W = 2.83 * V
150 G = W/.1
160 PRINT G
170 END
```

COMMAND STRUCTURES

Each of the commands which are illustrated above, regardless of which language they are written in, contains three major components, the output command, the listener's address, and the message itself. The output command is an inherent part of the syntax as specified by the manufacturer of the controller. We have seen that this can be somewhat different between one controller and another. The words OUTPUT, PRINT, and wrt all mean the same thing, but only to the individual controller language of which they are a part. The address portion of the command is also unique with each manufacturer.

The message part of the command, however, is always the same regardless of which manufacturer's controller is transmitting on the bus. The string "F2R3S1T0," sent to a typical GPIB digital voltmeter, is part of the syntax required by the DVM. Any deviation from this would not result in the desired message being transmitted to the meter, since that instrument will recognize only its own format.

CONTROLLER TIME-OUT PERIOD

The GPIB interface system is designed with a handshake protocol so that message transfer on the bus can proceed only as fast as the slowest addressed listener can accept data. This is a very important feature of this system, since it prevents multi-acceptance of the same ASCII character by a fast listener while a slow one is receiving the same data. The NDAC handshake line is used to indicate the acceptance of data by all addressed listeners, and the slowest one will hold this line low (true) until it has properly accepted the data. Only when the line is released by all listeners will the interface system proceed to the next business at hand.

Under this restraint, the controller (and all other instruments and devices on the bus) is powerless to proceed with communications until the NDAC line goes high. If a device malfunctions and cannot accept data, the communications on the bus can come to a complete halt when using controllers which have an interface time-out period of infinity. This problem is eliminated in some controllers which have a time-out period set by either default or by a Set Interface Time-out command in the software.

The time-out value tells the controller how long it should wait for a handshake cycle to be completed. If an instrument malfunction should cause the handshake cycle to be delayed beyond this allotted time, the communication between the controller and that device is aborted, thus permitting the interface system to continue with its normal communications.

Under normal operation of the bus it is also possible that a slow instrument can cause the handshake cycle to be delayed longer than usual, possibly by a command which requires the instrument to perform a complex, time-consuming task that delays cycle completion. If the controller can be programmed for a set time-out period of perhaps 1 second, the speed of communication on the bus will not be slowed in most cases. When the software program has been completed and debugged, this time-out period may be able to be set to a lower value.

Sample programs illustrating the time-out function will be found in Appendix I.

SERVICE REQUEST INTERRUPTS

Service Request Interrupts are used by devices and instruments on the bus to alert the controller to a change in status (including power-up) or the existence of a problem. One of the five management lines, identified as SRQ, is shared by all instruments on the bus and is used for this purpose. Any unit on the bus can assert an SRQ on this line to force an interruption in the current sequence of events. There is no way for the controller to determine which device on the bus asserted the SRQ, so it must query all units in the form of a serial or parallel poll to determine which unit required service. Some controllers will simply generate an error message when an SRQ is received if they have not been programmed to respond to the request. Others will ignore an SRQ unless they are explicitly told what to do.

Since the SRQ line can be asserted for such conditions as power on, warning messages, operational errors, and equipment malfunction, it is generally good practice to include a routine in the software to handle these conditions when they occur. Of course, there is no way to know when such a request is going to be generated by a device on the line, so some sort of asynchronous command, such as ON SRQ THEN 2000 must be written into the software. This statement, used in Tektronix 4050 BASIC, transfers control to a subroutine at line 2000 when an SRQ occurs. When the program executes the ON SRQ command, transfer does not take place at that time. Instead, a link is established in the program so that later, when an SRQ actually occurs, the program is suspended and the subroutine at line 2000 is initiated. A RETURN statement at the end of the subroutine returns the program to the point at which it was interrupted, so that it may continue.

When the controller receives an SRQ interrupt, it must determine which unit on the bus requested service, since the SRQ line is shared with all units on the bus. This process is termed polling, and the IEEE-488 system allows either serial poll or parallel poll as the method by which the controller determines which unit requires service.

When the parallel poll is executed, up to eight units on the bus are assigned a unique line on the eight GPIB data lines. Then, when the controller asks for a parallel poll, the device which asserted SRQ places its status bit on its assigned line. (Should there be more than eight units on the bus, parallel poll must be done in two or more groups.) Once the unit which requires service has been identified, the software determines what action should be taken. This depends on the applications program, as determined by the test engineer.

If the serial poll is implemented in the program, the instruments are polled one at a time. In this case each instrument and device on the bus can provide a fairly detailed status report, since 8 bits are available to each instrument to encode its status. When a serial poll is initiated by the controller, the SRQ status of each instrument is automatically cleared when it is polled.

Controllers usually are able to provide a high-level command which implements either the parallel poll, serial poll, or both. For example, in the 4050 BASIC language, the poll command POLL N,S ; 8, 5, 7 will cause the controller to read the status byte from devices with addresses 8, 5, and 7 in that sequence, but it stops as soon as it has detected the device asserting SRQ. When that happens, the status byte is returned in S and the position of the asserting device is stored in N. In the above example, if device 7 was asserting SRQ, the number 3 would be returned in N. Note that the sequence of polling occurs in the order written in the POLL command and not in numerical order.

The IEEE-488 document defines only 1 bit of the status byte which is set when an instrument is asserting SRQ and is cleared otherwise or when it is polled by the serial poll. Since the definition of the other 7 bits of the status byte is left to the discretion of the manufacturer of the instrument or device, it can be seen that it might be quite difficult to program the software to decode the multitude of possible status codes from many different manufacturers.

Some manufacturers have defined standards which define the SRQ status byte for all instruments that they manufacture, which can greatly simplify the programming task for the test engineer. In the Tektronix Codes and Formats standard, for example, a set of codes is defined which all Tektronix instrument will report in the case of an SRQ. Table 6-5 illustrates the various status bytes along with the type of condition they represent.

Some GPIB instruments have been designed to allow a "mask" to be applied to all serial polls. This feature allows the software engineer the option of programming into the system a command which will cause the instrument to ignore the poll. This is illustrated in Table 6-6, a typical serial poll response byte from the Wavetek model 278 function generator.

In Table 6-6 the SRQ status conditions can be masked by a command from the controller. In the case of the Wavetek generator described, the command XQ, followed by a value 0 through 255, selects the conditions under which the generator will assert the SRQ line and RSV bit. The equivalent binary value of the number following the XQ command is the mask for the serial poll response byte. A 1 in the binary value means that the condition is selected to be recognized; a 0 allows the generator to ignore the condition.

PRIMARY ADDRESS

All GPIB devices are assigned an address, from 0 to 30, by means of a set of switches or jumpers. Usually the manufacturer of the

Table 6-5.   Tektronix standard for status bytes returned in response to a serial poll.

Status Byte	Condition
011X 0000	The device is reporting an error but not identifying it. The controller must send ERR? to determine what it is.
011X 0001	Command error resulting from a message that can't be lexically analyzed.
011X 0010	Execution error. The device can analyze the command but cannot execute it, such as setting a meter out of range.
011X 0011	Internal error such as may be caused by a malfunction within the device.
011X 0100	Power failure. Alerts the controller to possible defective data.
011X 0101	Execution error warning. The controller is alerted that the device is executing a command but a problem may exist, such as taking a measurement out of range.
011X 0110	Internal error warning. The device indicates that it has an internal error but is continuing to function anyway.
000X 0000	This byte is returned when the device has nothing out of the ordinary to report.
010X 0000	SRQ query request. The device asks the controller to send SRQ? to determine why it is requesting service.
010X 0001	Power on. Sent when a device has finished a power on sequence and has come on the bus.
010X 0010	Operation complete. Alerts the controller that some task has been completed and it is ready for another command.

Note that the "X" in the byte is 1 when the device has asserted SRQ, and cleared when it has not.

instrument or device will select a specific address for all like instruments, and this may be changed to any other allowable address by the user. Although the address selection can be any number from 0 to 30, it actually represents two addresses: the talk address (MTA) and the listen address (MLA). When the controller wants a unit to listen to a message, it will assert the listen address. Similarly, when it wants the unit to talk, it will send the talk address.

Table 6-6.   Typical SRQ status byte generated by a function generator.

Byte	Bit Decimal Position	Bit Name	Bit Description
00000001	1	Program error	Indicates an error in the software
00000010	2	Output protection circuit	Indicates that output protection has been tripped.
00000100	4	Fuse	Indicates that fuse has been blown.
00001000	8	Battery	Indicates that battery is low.
00010000	16	Reference	Indicates that generator is not locked to the reference signal.
00100000	32	Undefined	Undefined
01000000	64	RSV	Request for service.
10000000	128	SRQ	Front panel SRQ key has been pressed.

The actual listen and talk addresses of the GPIB device are offset by a specific number from the switch or jumper selected primary address. in accordance with the sixth and seventh bits on the data lines. Adding 32 to the primary address generates the listen address; adding 64 generates the talk address. It is usually not necessary for the programmer to write the software with the necessary offset for the desired listen or talk address since most controllers in use today provide high-level commands which automatically set bits 6 and 7 and generate the correct addresses. For example, the HP-BASIC command OUTPUT 703 will address a device with a primary address of 3 to listen, by sending the listen address 35. The command ENTER 703 will address that same device to talk by sending the talk address 67. In each of these commands the HP-BASIC language requires that the select code, 7 for HP-IB controllers, precede the device address.

It is important to note that in any given GPIB system no two instruments may share the same address. Since 31 addresses are available, there is no problem in setting each instrument or device to its own unique address. If the system contains units from two or more different manufacturers, it is very possible that the GPIB address selected by the manufacturers may be duplicated. Should this occur, one of the duplicate addresses must be changed to an unused one by resetting one or more of the address switches on one of the units.

SECONDARY ADDRESS

Although for most instruments one listen and one talk address is all that is necessary for that device to properly function on the GPIB, there is a provision in the interface system to allow multiple addressing, which permits the controller to go one step further into the instrument. This is referred to as a secondary address.

For example, it is possible to have a GPIB controlled power supply which may contain two or more plug-in boards to provide separate power sources which may be individually controlled via the bus. The power supply mainframe will be assigned the primary address so that the controller can access that instrument when required. Once the mainframe has been so accessed, the secondary address will then be used to address the desired plug-in board. In this way a GPIB controlled instrument or device can be designed so that the controller has the capability of reaching into the instrument to control a specific portion of it.

When addressing a GPIB controlled device with a secondary address, the controller command will contain both address codes, usually separated by a punctuation character. For example, the

Fluke BASIC command to address a designated section of a listener with a primary address 10 and a secondary address 4 is:

```
PRINT @ 10 : 4, A$
```

This command addresses the device and transmits the contents of string A$ to the portion of it identified as secondary address 4.

Chapter 7

TEKTRONIX Codes
and Formats

Although the first major step in the GPIB interface system was taken in 1975 when the IEEE published its 488 standard, designing an interface system using GPIP instruments and suitable software was a major task because of the differences in programming requirements for each manufacturer. Tektronix saw the need for compatibility between all instruments on the bus and has took the next step by adopting a standard which is called Codes and Formats. The purpose of this standard is to define device-dependent message formats to enhance the compatibility between instruments on the bus, regardless of who manufactured them. By using the Tektronix Codes and Format standard, the cost and time required to develop applications software is substantially reduced. A standard system of programming requirements allows the software engineer to generate the required programs in much less time than would be otherwise required . In addition, the resulting device-dependent commands are easier to understand.

An offshoot of this philosophy provided manufacturers of GPIB instruments the impetus to design user-friendly products so that the required commands were easy to understand and the operation of the system was tolerant of operator errors.

As a result of the Codes and Format standard, instrument manufacturers have realized many advantages including reduced labor costs, more efficient use of engineering skills, and improved techniques through the reduction of human errors and more accurate, repeatable measurements.

COMPATIBILITY BETWEEN GPIB INSTRUMENTS

One of the first questions which must be addressed is the "language" which must be used by all instruments and devices on the bus when transferring numerical data. The IEEE-488.1 standard defines the system by which the message and data transfer takes place, but it allows the instrument designer the option of selecting the format. For example, if a voltmeter takes a voltage reading which must be transferred on the bus, it would be possible to transmit the information encoded in BCD or ASCII. Since the information is transferred in a bit parallel, byte serial fashion, another option arises: Should the data be transferred with the most significant digit first, last, or some other way? Figure 7-1 illustrates three possible ways in which measurement data can be transferred. It can easily be seen that if an instrument encodes data in BDC and the controller understands only ASCII, there can be a very cumbersome problem to enable the devices to communicate with each other.

Because almost all GPIB instruments today use ASCII coded characters to send and receive data, the Tektronix Codes and Formats standard has selected ASCII coding as standard. In addition, it utilizes the ANSI X3.42 standard which states that there are three types of numbers — integers, reals, and reals with exponents. These must be transmitted with the most significant character first.

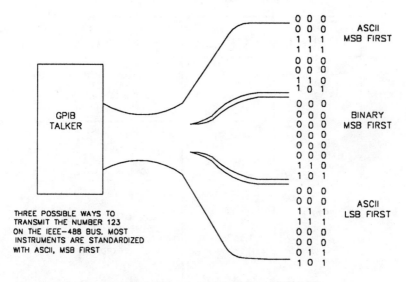

Figure 7-1.   Example of three ways to transmit the number 123.

Figure 7-2 is a tabulation of the three different types of numbers together with the restrictions on their format.

Although the format shown in Figure 7-2 has been defined by the Codes and Formats standard, the use of such data has not. Such a number may represent a voltage, a frequency, or any other data which can be generated by a GPIB device. To identify this data, it should be preceded by a "header" such as voltage, frequency, etc. When more than one type of data is transmitted such as might be obtained by a phase angle voltmeter, each set should have its own header (voltage and phase) and there should be a semicolon separating them. When one type of data contains several measurements such as repeated voltage readings, the data may be preceded by the header and each set of data separated by a comma. Figure 7-3 illustrates several types of messages containing multiple data which could be sent over the bus.

TYPE	EXAMPLES	RESTRICTIONS
INTEGERS	123 + 740 − 156 + 0	VALUE OF "0" MUST NOT CONTAIN A MINUS SIGN
REAL NUMBERS	+ 45.71 7.69 − 00045.1 0.000	RADIX POINT SHOULD BE PRECEDED BY AT LEAST ONE DIGIT VALUE OF "0" MUST NOT CONTAIN A MINUS SIGN.
REAL NUMBERS WITH EXPONENTS	75.2E − 2 − 1.657E + 1 + 00.00E + 00	VALUE OF "0" MUST BE WRITTEN AS A REAL NUMBER FOLLOWED BY A ZERO EXPONENT

Figure 7-2.   Three types of numbers allowed in the codes and formats standard.

The well-defined formats of data transfer over the bus, as described above, significantly enhance compatibility and communication among the instruments on the bus.

THE HUMAN INTERFACE

Since personnel with a limited range of skills may be called upon to be involved with a GPIB interface system, it is important that the commands which are directed to each instrument are easy to understand and as simple as possible. For example, if it is desired to program a power supply with a maximum output of 20 volts to 5 volts, it should not be necessary for the software to contain the

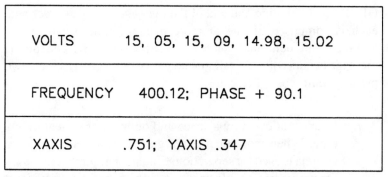

VOLTS	15, 05, 15, 09, 14.98, 15.02
FREQUENCY	400.12; PHASE + 90.1
XAXIS	.751; YAXIS .347

Figure 7-3.   Examples of multiple data that may be sent over the bus. Note that each data ID is preceded by an identifying header.

ratio 5/20 in the device dependent message. A far better method, allowing the power supply to compute its own required ratio from the command, would be to send the sequence VOLTS POSITIVE 20. Since most GPIB instruments manufactured today contain microprocessors, it is not a difficult task to ask the power supply to decode such a message and provide the correct output. This type of format makes it easy for the software engineer, but possibly more important it allows others who may come in contact with the program at a later date to easily understand what the program instructions are supposed to do.

The Codes and Formats standard adopted by Tektronix enhances instrument and controller compatibility not only with the devices themselves but with the people of widely divergent technical skills which must work with them.

DEVICE-DEPENDENT MESSAGE STRUCTURE

A device-dependent message represents a certain amount of information which is transmitted from one device to another on the

GPIB. The beginning and end of the message are clearly defined; each is composed of one or more message units separated by message unit delimiters such as a semicolon. The end of the message occurs when the talking device asserts EOI. There are two message unit types. These are:

1. Header followed by a space and optional argument of any type. When more than one argument follows a header, a comma is used for separation. Character arguments are used for programming information, and noncharacter arguments are used for measurement data.
2. Query message unit consisting of a character argument followed by a question mark. A typical query, VOLTS?, could be used to interrogate a voltmeter for its current reading.

In addition to numbers, the device-dependent message units can contain words which provide a specific instruction for an instrument to assume a desired mode. Such commands may be TRIGGER EXTERNAL, FUNCTION DC, etc. In these situations the first word of the command is considered to be a header and the remainder data, called the argument, which is different from a number. Other types of arguments are useful for various purposes. These may be:

1. String arguments. Used to send text to a display or printer
2. Binary block arguments. Used to send blocks of binary data of known length
3. End block. Used to send binary data of unknown length or format
4. Link arguments. Used to send certain types of instrument commands

Table 7-1 summarizes the allowable argument types which are specified by the Tektronix Codes and Formats standard.

CONVENTIONS

Although the IEEE-488 document defines the operating system between GPIB instruments, it does not guarantee compatibility between all such instruments and devices produced by different manufacturers. To provide well-defined operating conventions the Tektronix Codes and Formats standard requires that a message placed on the bus be a complete block of information. The purpose of this requirement is to ensure that all instruments which meet the Tektronix standard will be compatible with one another and no possibility of ambiguity will occur as a result of poor hardware design or software and human error. The block of information begins when a talking device starts sending data and ends when EIO is sent or received concurrently with the last data byte.

Without a well-defined system of message conventions it is possible that some components in a GPIB system would not work properly together. Suppose, for example, that the controller requests a voltage reading from a meter which then transmits the data followed by CR (carriage return) and LF (line feed). If the controller is designed to respond to the CR character alone as the end of the message, it will "hang up" at that point leaving the LF character in the meter, unsent. When the meter is asked to provide the next reading, the leftover LF character is sent first resulting in a message which is meaningless to the controller, and an error is indicated.

Since some GPIB instruments are capable of transmitting data in binary format which could conceivably take the form of the CR or LF characters, a standard way to end a message is to assert EOI when the last data byte of a message is sent. This prevents any

Table 7-1.   Examples and definitions of allowable argument types.

Argument Type	Example	Definition	Purpose
Character argument	Trigger	One alphabetic ASCII character optionally followed by any number of ASCII characters excluding space, comma, semicolon, and question mark.	To transfer alphanumeric data such as message headers, labels, & commands.
Non-character argument	Number -123.4	A numeric value in any of the formats shown in Table 1.	To send numeric values in ASCII format.
String argument	"Connect meter"	Single or double quote followed by any number of ASCII characters, and a closing quote identical to the opening one.	To send ASCII text to a display, printer, etc.
Binary block argument	%(2 bytes) (binary data) (check sum)	% followed by 2 byte binary integer specifying the number of data bytes, plus an 8 bit checksum.	To transfer large amounts of numeric data such as waveforms.
Link argument	TEST:12	Character argument followed by a colon, followed by a value represented in any of the above argument types.	To attach a label to another argument.
End block argument	@ABCDEF E O I	@ followed by a block of data with EOI concurrent with the last data byte. End block can be only the last argument in a message.	To send a block of data when the amount or format is unknown.

possible false interpretation of data sent in binary form as the end of a message. The Tektronix Codes and Formats standard states that instruments sending messages must assert EOI concurrently with the last byte of the message.

There are other problems which may occur when instruments execute each individual command as received. A serious problem can occur, for example, when a programmable power supply capable of producing relatively high voltages is commanded to deliver a low voltage with a specified current limit followed by another command for a higher voltage at a lower current limit. With poor message handling capability, it is possible that the power supply will deliver the higher voltage at the current limit set from the previous command, because it has not yet received the new current limit. This could have disastrous results in the event that the load cannot sustain the excessive current limit. Proper programming should have set the new current limit before changing to the higher voltage. It is far better to design the power supply to execute such commands only when the whole message is received and accepted. The Tektronix standard prevents such an occurrence since it requires that the listener not execute any command until the entire message is received and terminated by the EOI line.

It is also important to clarify the message sequence further. If an instrument sending data is interrupted by the controller such as during a serial poll, it should continue with that message when it becomes a talker again. Thus, a message begins when a device enters the active talker state for the first time or following a previously sent EOI and ends when EOI is asserted concurrently with the last data byte.

When a device is instructed to talk, it should always say something, even if it has nothing to say. It should send a null message consisting of a byte of all 1s, concurrent with EOI. This tells the listener that no meaningful data is forthcoming, and it prevents the bus from being held up while the controller waits for data that does not exist.

Table 7-2.   Serial poll status byte definition.

Abnormal Conditions	Status Byte
ERR query requested	011X 0000
Command error	011X 0001
Execution error	011X 0010
Internal error	011X 0011
Power failure	011X 0100
Execution error warning	011X 0101
Internal error warning	011X 0110

Normal Conditions	
No status to report	000X 0000
SRQ query request	010X 0000
Power on	010X 0001
Operation complete	010X 0010

A listening device should always handshake even if it is confused by a message that it does not understand or cannot execute. After EOI is received, it should send out a Service Request and report to the controller that nonsense has been received. The listener must not, under any circumstances, attempt to execute a command that it does not understand. Suppose, for example, that a programmable power supply is commanded with a message containing four O's instead of four zeros (a common human error). It could conceivably put out its maximum voltage instead of the intended 0 volts, with disastrous results. This scenario cannot occur with instruments designed under the Tektronix Codes and Formats standard.

STATUS BYTES

Except for bit 7 (binary position 64), IEEE-488.1 does not specify the meaning of the bits of the status byte which is sent to the controller in response to a serial poll. Bit 7 is asserted when a device has requested service.

Since there is a need for instruments to report certain types of operating conditions or errors, the Tektronix Codes and Formats standard has established a status byte convention. This is summarized in Table 7-2. One common requirement is the need to report if an instrument is busy or ready. Bit 5 has been reserved for this purpose. A second need is to report if an instrument is experiencing an abnormal condition. Bit 4 is reserved for this. In Table 7-2 bit 5 has been shown as X, since it could be either a 1 or 0 depending if the instrument is in a busy or ready state.

In some instruments there may be more complex conditions which must be reported in the status byte. In such cases, bit 8 may be asserted. This will alert the controller that the status byte received in response to the serial poll is not the ordinary type as illustrated in Table 7-2, but is particular to that instrument.

QUERIES

Although the serial poll status byte can be used to transmit much information concerning the condition of a device on the bus, it may be necessary to send more details to the controller. This is accomplished through "queries." A talker on the bus will usually send measurement data when addressed to talk by the controller. In order to receive information other than measurement data, the controller can query the instrument in the form of a header, followed by a question mark. The following are examples of queries and their uses:

ERR? This is used to determine detailed error conditions in an instrument. The response to this query can be a number which is coded to indicate the particular problem that is being experienced by the instrument.

SET? This query is used by the controller to command the instrument to send its present settings and other current status information. If this information is sent back to the instrument at a later time, it can return the instrument to the same state as when the SET? query was received. This feature makes it possible to develop a program which enables the instrument's front panel controls to be used as an input to the controller.

ID? This query forces an instrument to identify itself by sending information such as model type and firmware version back to the controller. Such a feature is useful to identify a particular instrument in the field.

COMPATIBILITIES

As more and more "intelligent" instruments and devices become available, it is obvious that the necessity for compatibility between the controller and various instruments on the bus is greater than ever before. Any device with GPIB capability that contains microprocessors or other advanced circuitry should be easier to use, not more difficult. To this end, the Tektronix Codes and Formats standard has specified several requirements which will enhance the compatibility between controller and slave devices. Such compatibility must, of course, include human and system considerations. The following are examples of conventions adopted by the standard:

1. Instruments should always send numbers in the formats described earlier. However, when the instrument or device is required to receive numbers, it should do so in a "forgiving" manner. For example, although negative zero should never be transmitted on the bus, it should be accepted as zero. Any number which is in scientific notation format should adhere to the ANSI X3.42 standard, which specifies the inclusion of the decimal point. Any number sent without a decimal point should be received with an implied decimal point following the least significant digit. Additionally, if a number is received which has greater precision than the listener can handle, it should be rounded off and not truncated. This will enhance system accuracy.

2. A listener should always recognize spaces and commas as argument delimiters. Multiple spaces or commas should not be considered to be delimiters for null arguments. This is an important convention since some controllers generate spaces and send them on the bus.

3. It should not matter if headers and character arguments are received or sent in upper- or lower-case. Such a convention makes it easier for both programmer and human operator of the interface bus.

4. Headers and character arguments which are sent by any instrument should always conform to the corresponding front panel controls of that device. This convention will go a long way in reducing confusion and will help in understanding the programming and operation of the bus.

The above conventions are designed to make instruments more friendly in their programming requirements, which will be greatly appreciated by those who are not fully experienced with the interface bus.

There are other features which can be included in instruments that are designed to the Tektronix standard. One of these is the Service Request function and corresponding status bytes which are returned in response to a serial poll. An important feature of this capability is to inform the controller that an instrument has received a command which it cannot execute, or that it is experiencing an internal malfunction. This is important when such an instrument is left unattended. It may also be possible that there could be some measurement sequences which should not be interrupted by an SRQ, such as when a sensitive, time-dependent measurement is being taken. During such a sequence, the command RQS OFF can be sent to disable the Service Request feature. To resume, the command RQS ON would be sent.

Another consideration is the response to the Device Trigger (DT) command. It may be desired to have an immediate response to this command, or possibly only the instrument set-up for the Group Execute Trigger command is desired. To have an immediate response the message DT OFF is sent; to defer execution of commands the message DT ON is sent.

The conventions discussed provide friendlier instruments and enhance compatibility with all instruments on the bus. Without well-defined codes and formats and without easy-to-understand commands, instruments can be difficult to program and use. Using the Tektronix Codes and Formats standard allows all devices to be friendly, compatible, and easy to use. This goes a long way in making the IEEE-488 bus the powerful and valuable tool that it was meant to be.

Chapter 8

Hewlett-Packard PC Interface Bus

OVERVIEW

Although the Hewlett-Packard Interface Bus, otherwise known as the GPIB, has attained international standard status, HP has continued in its development of other interface systems which could satisfy the growing need for device communication, especially with regard to low-cost portable instrumentation which could be used with the personal computer. One of these, the Hewlett-Packard Interface Loop (HP-IL), was developed to perform the interface function for battery powered instruments, but its data transfer rate was far too slow to be considered for PC instrumentation. The first group of instruments which was designed to work with the personal computer did not use the HP-IL system. Instead, a new interface system called Personal Computer Interface Bus (PCIB), was developed for a special line of instruments which were unlike previous designs; they were designed specifically to be controlled by the personal computer. Figure 8-1 illustrates the difference in architecture between the GPIB and PCIB systems.

119

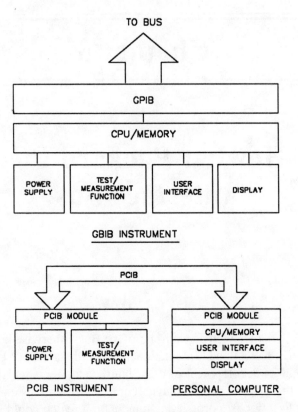

Figure 8-1.   Difference in architecture of the GPIB and PCIB systems.

One of the major objectives of the PCIB system was low cost, which could be attained by allowing the display screen of the computer to serve as the front panel of each of the instruments of the interface system. The instruments would have no front panel controls or displays, and the PC monitor would simulate the front panel of each of the instruments as required. A touch screen, mouse, or curser would be used to change the settings of the instruments.

The PCIB system is designed to provides a high data rate to enable the PC screen to update quickly enough for real time oscilloscope displays. An additional feature of the system is the capability to provide electrical isolation between the instruments or peripherals and the computer as might be required in a sensitive test setup. To this end the PCIB has been designed as a dual interface system which can provide both a high data rate and electrical isolation, but not simultaneously.

Since the slave instruments in the PCIB system have no front panel controls and are designed to use the computing power of the host PC instead of built-in microprocessors, they can be manufactured at lower cost than similar instruments which would be used in a GPIB system. Up to eight instruments can be served by one card plugged into the computer, and additional plug-in cards allow eight more additional instruments. Specially designed software ties instrument control closely to the MS-DOS operating system of the HP Vectra and IBM PC family of computers.

SYSTEM OBJECTIVES

Since the personal computer has proven to be a capable and cost effective instrument controller, the PCIB system was designed to complement and enhance its price and performance capabilities. Certain objectives were thus attained in the design of the system. Some of these are:

1. Produce PCIB instruments which were low in manufacturing cost through the use of fewer components (50 percent or less) than traditional instruments.
2. Use an unshielded cabling scheme which could be easily configured by end users. This design would meet all the requirements of Hewlett-Packard and regulatory agency standards for electromagnetic compatibility (EMC) performance.

3. Have a data rate of at least 100,000 bytes per second to provide a reasonable update speed of the computer display.
4. Provide the capability to float instruments at line voltage potentials while maintaining stringent safety standards for both computer and instrumentation.
5. Maintain an interface power level of 1 watt or less. Lower operating power allows the use of battery operated equipment and usually results in a lower-cost instrument.
6. Support eight PCIB instruments with a single interface card placed in the computer expansion slot.

SYSTEM DESCRIPTION

The PC interface system is designed to have up to eight instruments connected to the bus with just one interface card plugged into the host computer's expansion slot. Additional cards permit increments of eight more instruments to be connected together in the system. Any mix of PC instrument modules is permitted.

The PCIB contains a register-oriented architecture in which each function and data location has an individual register associated with it. There are 16 directly addressable write registers and 16 directly addressable read registers assigned to each instrument on the bus. If required, expansion to a greater number of registers can be accomplished through the use of an indirect addressing scheme. System software provides the necessary commands which are required in a register-oriented system, thus relieving the user of these details. A simple communications protocol is used which contains just three message types: command, address, and data.

Since the system uses separate registers per function, it is not necessary for the PC instrument to process complicated codes and formats. Instead, the instrument accepts the data from the bus and directs it to the specified register, which causes the desired action to take place. Unlike the GPIB and HP-IL systems, the PC Instruments Bus does not rely on mnemonics which were used for the human operators and programmers to help them understand the commands and messages on the bus. In the PCIB system the human interface is provided in the software, permitting a standard approach to program commands.

Standard instrument operations such as initialize, enable, or disable output are implemented through the use of command messages. All such commands are single byte and can be directed to a single instrument (selected commands) or to all instruments simultaneously (universal commands). This capability is similar to that of the GPIB. Sixteen different commands are possible in the PCIB system.

Instruments in the PCIB system can be listeners, talkers, or both. Each unit has its own listen and talk addresses which are used by the computer to select the instrument to which a message is directed. Addresses are a single byte which also includes the register which is to be used for the data transfer. The host computer is always the source or recipient of all data transfers.

Data transfers are performed 1 byte at a time to or from a selected register in a form which can be directly used by the instrument. Thus, it is not translated to and from ASCII. This keeps the number of bytes smaller, reducing the overhead in each instrument. To perform high-speed, multiple byte transfers, the parallel communications channel is used.

PARALLEL COMMUNICATIONS CHANNEL

The parallel communications channel, illustrated in Figure 8-2, must be used whenever high-speed data transfer between instruments and computer is required. This mode of operation does not permit electrical isolation between units. Data rates up to 100,000 bytes per second are possible, depending upon the limitations of the host computer. A custom integrated circuit containing the output

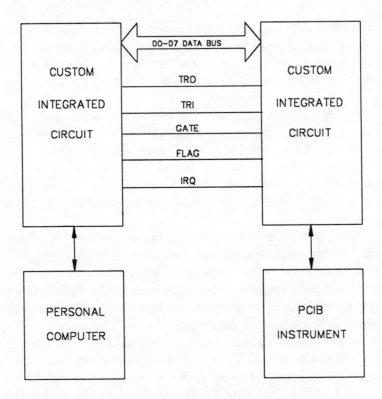

Figure 8-2.   PCIB parallel communications channel.

drivers are designed for limited rise and fall times of the logic levels
to help meet EMC requirements. This chip also implements the
protocol, system commands, and register decoding for the instruments of the bus.

As shown in Figure 8-2, the parallel communications channel
contains eight data lines, two transaction control lines TR0 and
TR1, two handshake lines GATE and FLAG, and an interrupt
request line. These 13 signal paths with their ground returns are part
of the 26 conductor cable which connects the host computer to the
instruments of the bus.

Table 8-1.   Definitions of encoding of transaction control lines TR0 and TR1

TR1	TR0	Definition
0	0	Reserved for future expansion
0	1	System command
1	0	Instrument address
1	1	Data byte

Unlike the GPIB, the PCIB uses a two-wire handshake system. These signal leads are identified as GATE and FLAG. GATE is asserted when data placed on the bus by the host computer is valid. During the command, address, and data operations, the selected instrument(s) uses the gate line to strobe the data byte off the bus. When a data byte is to be transmitted to the computer, the addressed instrument uses GATE to strobe the data out of the internal register of the instrument and onto the bus.

To complete the handshake sequence FLAG is asserted by the instrument in response to the GATE signal generated by the computer. When the FLAG signal is asserted, it indicates to the computer that the data byte has been accepted. FLAG is also used to indicate that data placed on the bus by the instrument is valid and can be accepted by the computer.

Two control lines, TR0 and TR1, provide a 2-bit transaction code for the current bus operation. This is illustrated in Table 8-1.

The logic level of the control lines, as indicated in Table 8-1, is used by the computer and instruments on the bus to determine how the data byte on the bus is to be interpreted. This code is valid during the time when GATE is asserted. Note that instruments must not respond to the reserved code, not even with a handshake. To do so would compromise any future use of this code.

The data bus consists of eight bidirectional lines which are used by the computer and instruments to place and receive 1 data byte at a time. Data provided by the computer is valid only when it asserts the GATE handshake signal. Data from the instruments is valid only when the GATE and FLAG handshake signals are asserted. Output drivers on the bus have been designed with limited slew rate outputs to help reduce radio frequency interference (RFI) from the unshielded cable of the bus. This also reduces the possibility of cross talk between the conductors of the bus. To improve rejection of noise and spurious responses from reflections, the input receivers of the computer and instruments have a built-in hysteresis characteristic.

As illustrated in Figure 8-2, an interrupt request signal line, IRQ, is included in the PCIB. This has a similar function as SRQ of the GPIB. It is used by the instruments of the bus to alert the computer that a condition has occurred which requires the attention of the host computer. Such a condition could be as simple as an indication that the instrument is ready for the next data byte or a more complex one such as a circuit failure. The nature of the interrupt request is instrument dependent, and the IRQ line is low true, which allows a wired OR configuration between instruments. The computer can determine that IRQ has been asserted by polling the status register of its interface card.

The interface circuits used in the parallel communications channel are mostly contained in a custom integrated circuit. This chip handles all the bus protocol and generates the master data strobe signals for the instrument registers. Included in this IC is the controlled rise and fall times circuitry as well as the interrupt generation and detection circuits. Figure 8-3 is a simplified diagram illustrating the built-in time constant which controls the rise and fall times of the output drivers.

The host computer interacts with the parallel channel by writing to I/O locations in its address space. Bus sequences are handled by the PCIB I/O drivers. To allow bus operations to be handled at the

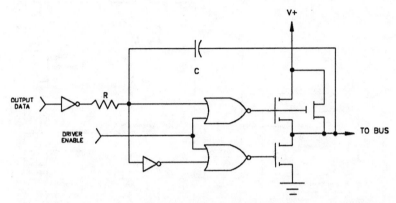

Figure 8-3.   Output driver circuit of custom IC illustrating the RC-controlled rise/fall time circuitry.

rate required by the addressed instrument, handshaking between the computer backplane and interface card is provided by an interface status register.

SERIAL COMMUNICATIONS CHANNEL

The serial communications channel, illustrated in Figure 8-4, is used for sensitive measurements if it is necessary to have electrical isolation between instruments and computer. This situation arises when the instruments must float at some potential above ground. This method of interface between units limits the data rate, so it can be used only when high speed is not a requirement of the system.

The serial bus uses two signals, TxD and RxD, for communication of all messages. These signal lines are part of the ribbon cable which also includes the parallel bus. TxD is the signal used by the computer to transmit command, address, and data messages. RxD is used by the instruments to acknowledge handshakes and return data and interrupt messages to the computer. Because multiple instruments must use the same two wires for transmitting and

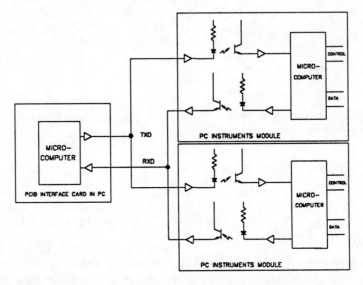

Figure 8-4.   PCIB serial communications channel. Note optoisolators in PC instuments module.

receiving messages, a new protocol had to be developed for serial communications. This is implemented by a single-chip microcomputer on the PCIB interface card, and in the instruments themselves.

Serial messages are transmitted in 12 bit frames as illustrated in Figure 8-5. The first bit is the start bit which synchronizes all instrument microcomputers to receive the transmitted data. The next two bits provide the transaction code, similar to that used in the parallel communications channel, which tells the instruments how to interpret the data which is to follow. The data byte which is to be transmitted comprise the next 8 bits of the serial sequence, and the last bit is used for parity check to ensure that the entire frame has been properly received.

When the serial frame is received by the instruments, it is examined by each to determine if any response is required. If a universal command is sent by the computer, all instruments of the

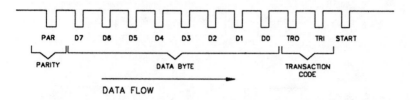

Figure 8-5.   PCIB serial frame illustrating flow of pulses.

bus will respond. When a listen address is sent, the specified listener will wait for the data byte which is to follow and will store it in the selected register. If a talk address is specified, the selected instrument will retrieve data from the selected register and transmit it back to the computer.

Each instrument's microcomputer also performs the handshake function to acknowledge receipt of a valid message. Figure 8-6 illustrates a handshake sequence which contains a valid data byte, a data byte which is verified valid on retransmission, and a system error.

If the parity of the message is correct, the addressed instrument returns a frame on RxD which contains a 2-bit set (double-bit width) indicating that good data was received. When the parity check fails,

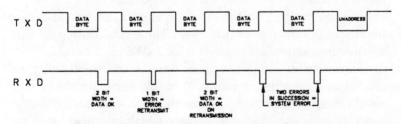

Figure 8-6.   Handshake sequence in serial communications channel showing valid data, valid data on retransmission, and system error.

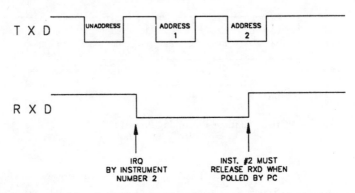

Figure 8-7.   IRQ sequence. When instrument requests service it pulls RXD low, and releases it when polled by host computer.

only 1 bit is returned, causing the sender to retransmit the previous frame. Should the parity check fail again on the retransmission, the message is aborted and an error signal is returned to the system.

When all instruments are unaddressed, any device which has a need for service and is capable of asserting IRQ will pull the RxD line low to alert the host computer that a request for service has been made. The computer responds by initiating a serial poll of all instruments. When the instrument which had requested service receives the poll, it releases the RxD line. This allows the system software to initiate the appropriate response to the request for service. Figure 8-7 illustrates the IRQ sequence.

All instruments on the bus are always aware of the current state of the system since they each receive all messages. During the time when no instruments are addressed, the RxD line is available to any instrument for use as an interrupt request line, which will pull it low if it has an interrupting condition. When the microcomputer on the interface card is alerted that an interrupt has occurred, the system software initiates a poll to determine which instrument requires service. When an address frame is sent on TxD, the instrument which initiated the interrupt is required to release the RxD line. This tells the host computer which instrument initiates IRQ and frees RxD so that it can be used as for handshake or data. The RxD line thus is capable of performing three tasks.

THE CUSTOM BUS INTERFACE IC

Since one of the requirements of the PCIB system is to use an easy-to-configure unshielded cable, it was necessary to design a custom integrated circuit (Figure 8-3) to eliminate problems which could be caused by signal crosstalk and radio frequency interference. Such a chip must contain bidirectional transceivers to the computer as well as the instruments of the bus.

The driving circuits are designed to have slew rates which are held to within predictable limits, regardless of the wide variation in load capacitance which can occur in different test setups. The maximum desired data rate, 100,000 bytes per second, fixes the slowest allowable rise and fall times. The maximum slew rate is constrained by strict Hewlett-Packard class B environmental requirements. NMOS technology was chosen over CMOS to avoid any possibility of latch-up.

The custom IC, packaged in a 48-pin dual-in-line package, requires a single 5-volt power supply and dissipates about 1/3 watt. It uses an internal negative substrate bias voltage generator.

The IC is required to implement three modes of operation: computer pass through, pod protocol, and test modes. In the pass through mode the chip is configured as a set of buffered, transparent bus transceivers, with a single input line controlling the direction of communication.

In the parallel communications bus the pod protocol mode invokes all the necessary logic for the instruments of the bus to communicate. These functions include asynchronous handshake, address selection and decoding, register control (command, read, and write), interrupt masking and status, and bus data transmission.

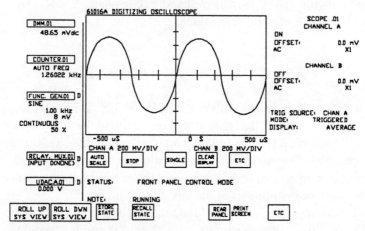

Figure 8-8.   Typical CRT display of host computer.

The test mode, used only at IC wafer test, configures a serial scan path through a 20-bit binary divider. This reduces the number of clock cycles required to test the sequential counter.

A typical PCIB might contain several of these custom IC chips. One chip will be located on the PC interface card and one in each of the instruments which operate on the parallel communications bus.

USING THE PCIB

A typical test setup of instruments under control of the PCIB might include an oscilloscope, digital voltmeter, function generator, and frequency counter in addition to the host computer. Since none of the instruments has an operational front panel, the test technician will control the system and view the simulated controls and displays of each instrument on the computer display CRT. Figure 8-8 illustrates a typical computer display for the test setup.

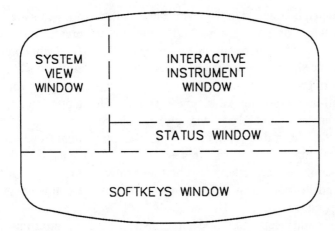

Figure 8-9.   Computer CRT is divided into four sections to allow system overview and control of selected instruments functions and settings.

The computer screen becomes the means by which the instruments are monitored and controlled. It is divided into four windows or sections (Figure 8-9). These are:

1. Soft keys or function keys which contain the function key blocks as in other PC programs.
2. Status window, a message area which provides prompts and error messages.
3. System view, an abbreviated view of all the instruments on the bus except that which is displayed in the main window.
4. Interactive instrument window, which provides a complete view of the desired instrument on the bus. From this window the functions and settings of the instrument can be viewed and controlled.

Note that in Figure 8-8 the main window of the display contains the oscilloscope waveform, with all pertinent scope information presented below and to the right. The smaller window, located on the left side of the computer CRT, contains an abbreviated display of several instruments in the setup. This allows the technician to view the status of these instruments while maintaining the instrument of greatest interest in the large window. By using the roll-up or roll-down function keys, any instrument on the bus (except the one displayed in the large window) can be seen.

If it is desired to bring one of the other instrument front panels into the main display area, this is easily accomplished by using a mouse or the cursor keys to point an arrow on the screen at the desired instrument or touching the screen if the computer is so equipped.

To modify settings, the desired instrument is brought into the main display window where the arrow on the screen can be pointed at the desired control. The function keys of the computer are then operated to increment or decrement the desired setting.

The PCIB system allows the user to save the front panel settings of all instruments for recall at a later time during manual or automatic operation. This is accomplished by operating the proper function keys of the computer and entering the MS-DOS directory and desired file name. The settings are stored in a similar manner to any program or data.

Chapter 9

The Hewlett-Packard Interface Loop

INTRODUCTION

The IEEE-488 Interface Bus (HP-IB) was developed to provide a means for various instruments and devices to communicate with each other under the direction of one or more master controllers. This interface system has been widely accepted all over the world, and there are currently more than 4000 different instruments and devices which have been designed for use in this powerful and elegant system.

The HP-IB was originally intended to support a wide range of instruments and devices, from the very fast to the very slow. However, since its inception, technology has spawned a wide proliferation of medium-speed, low-power, low-cost instrumentation which also had a very real need to be operated in an automatic test system such as the HP-IB. To satisfy this requirement, the Hewlett-Packard Company developed a new interface system to reflect and support the trends in electronic technology. One of these

135

systems is called the Hewlett-Packard Interface Loop (HP-IL), which is a low-cost, low-power alternative to the HP-IB system.

Although HP-IL and HP-IB provide the same basic functions in interfacing controllers, instruments, and peripherals, they differ in many respects. HP-IL is suitable for use in low-power, portable applications because of its very low power requirements. In general, it is not practical to operate the HP-IB from battery power. Because HP-IL instruments have just moderate performance as opposed to HP-IB devices, they generally are much lower in cost. The HP-IL maximum data rate is 20K bytes per second. This is a high rate compared to RS 232C, but much slower than HP-IB.

Cable length is generally not a problem with HP-IL; up to 100 meters separation between instruments, using shielded twisted pairs, is possible. HP-IB requires extender hardware to exceed 20 meters between devices.

It is possible to assemble a system which includes both HP-IB and HP-IL devices through the use of an HP-IB/HP-IL interface. One such unit is provided by the Hewlett-Packard Company, model HP 82169A Interface. The controller in a combined system using the HP Interface can be either an HP-IB or HP-IL device.

HP-IL OVERVIEW

The HP-IL is a serial interface which uses a pair of wires, usually in the form of a twisted pair, to transmit commands, messages, and data from one unit to another. As with the HP-IB system, there are three types of devices in HP-IL: listeners, talkers, and controllers. In any given HP-IL system there can be only one active controller at a time, but it is also possible to have a simple interface which contains one talker and one listener, and no controller. Figure 9-1 is an illustration of a simple HP-IL system containing a controller and three slave devices. This system can also be described as a ring or loop interface.

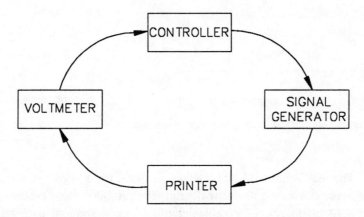

Figure 9-1.   Simple HP-IL system showing message path around the loop.

In this loop interface, information travels 1 bit at a time from one unit to the another, in sequence around the loop, until it returns to the originating device. Suppose, for example, that the controller in Figure 9-1 wanted to send a command to the voltmeter. Since the direction of message transmission is shown clockwise, the message must pass through the signal generator and printer before it reaches the voltmeter, where it is stored in memory. The data, meanwhile, continues around the loop to the controller where it can be compared to that which was sent out, to check for errors and prove its validity.

HP-IL FEATURES

The HP-IL system will support a total of 11 devices on a single loop using standard single-byte addresses. Provision has been made to use an extended form of addressing which involves 2-byte addresses. This permits the interface to support up to 960 devices.

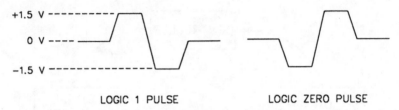

LOGIC 1 PULSE   LOGIC ZERO PULSE

Figure 9-2.   HP-IL transmission code waveshape.

The maximum data rate, using a shielded twisted pair of wires between devices, is theoretically limited to 20,000 bytes per second and is not affected by cable length. Since the actual data rate depends upon the maximum speed that a slave device can accept or transmit data, it would not be unususal to have a transmission speed of one tenth of the theoretical maximum; 2K bytes per second is equivalent to transmitting about half an 8 1/2 by 11 page of text per second.

Figure 9-2 illustrates the HP-IL three-level transmission code, in which a logic 1 is represented by a pulse of positive 1.5 volts followed by a negative pulse of -1.5 volts. Conversely, a logic 0 consists of a negative pulse of -1.5 volts follwed by a positive pulse of 1.5 volts. When there is no activity on the line, the voltage between the twisted pair remains at zero.

The electrical diagram of an HP-IL transmission path is shown in Figure 9-3. The line is electically isolated from the devices of the HP-IL by means of a pulse transformer, which provides level translation as well as isolation. Drivers and receivers are two wire balanced pair circuits. If a simple two-wire cable (zip cord) is connected between units, the maximum allowable distance is 10 meters. A twisted shielded pair permits the maximum distance to be 100 meters.

Additional features of the HP-IL system include a power-down or standby mode of operation in which the controller can place devices "to sleep" and wake them when necessary to perform a

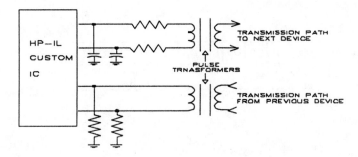

Figure 9-3.   Block diagram of HP-IL transmission line driver and receiver circuits.

required task. This can be a very important consideration when using battery-powered equipment.

HP-IL controllers may also incorporate an auto-addressing feature in which addresses are automatically assigned by the controller. This feature allows the user to add devices to the loop without worrying about setting address switches.

One of the features of the HP-IL system is the ability to collect data using a portable device and then bring the unit into the office or laboratory to transfer the information to the HP-IL system. This feature can be very advantageous for taking inventory, meter readings, market research, and any other requirement for which data must be assimilated at a remote location.

HP-IL MESSAGE STRUCTURE

The structure of an HP-IL message is depicted in Figure 9-4. It consists of 11 bits, three of which contain control information and the remainder data or commands. The HP-IL specification requires that all units of the interface speak the same language, and it defines a common set of messages that all devices in the system must understand.

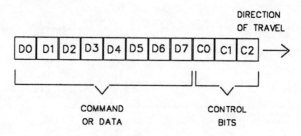

Figure 9-4.   HP-IL message structure.

This 11-bit message travels through the loop, with bit C2 being sent first. If a particular message pertains to the device that receives it, a local copy will usually be made and the message retransmitted to the next unit on the loop. This speeds up the overall throughput and allows execution to occur concurrently when more than one unit must respond.

Bit C2 is the first bit sent in the message, and it serves as a synchronizing or start bit, since the message is an asynchronous event. An additional function of C2 is to indicate to a device if the D0 to D7 bits of the message contain data (C2 = 0) or a Command, Ready or Identify message (C2 = 1).

Bit C1, in nondata frames, is set to 0 when the message is a Command or Ready frame and to 1 when an Identify frame is sent. In a data message, C1 is used to indicate that the byte is the last in a logical group.

Bit C0 is the service request bit in Data or Identify frames and is used to alert the controller that a device needs service as soon as possible. If C2 and C1 are 1 and 0 respectively, C0 indicates that that the message is a Command (C0 = 0) or Ready (C0 = 1) frame.

Figure 9-5 illustrates the HP-IL message hierarchy. The categories or classes of messages are based on the coding of the C2, C1, and C0 bits in the message frame and define a logical and convenient method of implementing the HP-IL messages in the software.

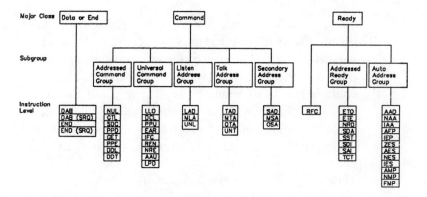

Figure 9-5.   HP-IL message hierarchy.

INTERFACE FUNCTIONS

A group of functions identified as primary interface functions are require for all devices which are intimately related to the primary HP-IL roles of listener, talker, or controller. These functions are:

1. Receiver (R). All units on the loop must be capable of the Receiver function since every device must be capable of listening to messages to determine if it is the intended recipient or should simply retransmit it to the next listener. The receiver function does not perform the retransmission of the message; this is provided by the driver interface function.

2. Driver (D). All devices must implement the driver function, since most received messages will require retransmission on the loop.

3. Listener (L). This function is required only for those units which will function as listeners on the loop, and it is active when the device has been addressed as a listener. Note the difference between the receiver function, which may merely

direct the driver to retransmit a message, and the listener function, which must accept messages from the acceptor handshake logic to be used by the instrument itself.

4.   Source Handshake (SH). Devices that operate as a talker or controller on the loop must be implemented with the source handshake function, since messages will originate within these units. This function receives messages to be transmitted from the device and directs the driver function to perform the actual transmission.

5.   Talker (T). The talker function permits a device to transmit data and status information on the loop. This capability is not activated until the unit receives its Talk Address (TAD) message. Data cannot be sent until the Send Data (SDA) message is received. This function also has the resposibility of generating the End of Transmission (EOT) message after data and status transmissions are completed.

6.   Controller (C). Any device on the loop which implements the controller function will be able to generate the Command (CMD), Ready (RDY), and Identify (IDY) messages. It will also be able to check the loop for service requests and perform parallel polls. Although there can be more than one device on the loop capable of acting as the controller, only one can be active at a time. This responsibility is passed between controllers using the Take Control (TCT) command. Only one device, however, is designated as system controller, which has the responsibility of assuming control at power-up and is the only device on the loop whch can source the Interface Clear (IFC) message.

Device-control interface functions are associated with the actual functions of the devices on the loop rather than with the primary functions described above. These functions are:

1. Power-down. This optional function is activated in a device when the Loop Power Down (LPD) message is sent by the controller. The LPD message is not specifically addressed to any one or group of units; any device which does not implement this function merely ignores it and passes it to the next device on the loop. A unit which assumes a power-down mode may place itself in a low-powered state or completely shut down as designed by the manufacturer of the equipment. All devices that respond to the power-down command must monitor the loop at all times to be able to receive and react to the "wake-up" command from the controller. Any activity on the loop after the LPD message automatically returns all powered-down devices to their normal state. The power-down feature is useful when battery powered equipment is being used on the loop.

2. Device clear (DC). This optional function may be implemented in a device two different ways. The DC1 subset of this function allows the instrument to be cleared to a known state (determined by the device manufacturer) when the Device Clear (DCL) message is received. The DC2 subset allows the additional capability of permitting the device to be selectively cleared by the controller when the Selected Device Clear (SDC) message is sent.

3. Remote Local (RL). This optional function permits a device to respond to either its own front panel controls or to instructions by the controller. This feature is useful when a device's functions or settings must be frequently changed during the course of a test sequence. An extended version of this function provides a lockout feature which deactivates the front panel controls when the Local Lockout (LLO) message is received. This prevents an operator from altering an instrument's setting during the test.

There are additional interface functions which may be included in a device. These are of a general nature, dealing with the loop itself rather than with any particular device function. They include:

1. Automatic address. This optional function allows a device to be assigned an address as directed by the controller. There are no subsets to this function, but two other interface functions provide a variation of the auto address feature. These are auto-extended (AE) and auto-multiple (AM). The auto-extended function allows a device to store the address directed by the controller, increment it, and pass it to the next device in the loop. The auto-multiple function allows each function in a device to be assigned a separate loop address.

2. Device Dependent (DD). This optional function allows a device to respond to a message when the meaning of that message is entirely dependent upon the device itself. Before a unit can respond to such a message, it must first be addressed as a talker or listener by means of the DDL (device-dependent listener) or DDT (device-dependent talker) command. Since this function provides a simple way to control device activity, it will probably be implemented in most HP-IL devices.

3. Service Request. This optional function allows a unit to request service from the controller by setting the service request byte in a Data or End (DOE), or Identify (IDY) message. Any device so implemented must also be capable of being addressed as a talker so that it can respond with a status byte when the controller responds to the service request with a polling operation.

4. Parallel poll. This optional function allows a unit to respond to a parallel poll from the controller by returning 1 bit of status information within the IDY polling message. Any such device so implemented must be capable of being a

listener and must respond to the Parallel Poll Enable (PPE), Parallel Poll Disable (PPD), Parallel Poll Unconfigure (PPU), and Identify (IDY) messages.

COMMAND GROUP MESSAGES

The Command Group messages are those which are sourced by the controller to establish initial operating conditions on the loop and to change operating modes of the listeners in accordance with the requirements of the test sequence. These are:

1. Interface Clear (IFC). The IFC message is typically sent around the loop at the time of power-up of the system to ensure that all devices are programmed into a predefined state. When the message has completed its trip around the loop, it informs the controller to send the Ready for Command (RFC) message to verify that all devices have completed the IFC command.

2. Device Clear (DCL). The Device Clear message can be used by the controller to reset a device to a predefined state. Not all units on the bus need to respond to this message. The Selected Device Clear (SDC) command may be sent to clear only those devices which have been addressed as listeners. This command is useful when there are many devices on the loop and the user wishes to clear only one or more selected units.

3. Loop Power-Down (LPD). This command provides a means for the user to conserve power by setting devices on the loop in a standby or idle state. This feature is very useful when one or more devices on the bus is powered by an internal battery.

4. Listen Address (LAD). This command is used by the controller to cause a selected device to become an active lis-

tener. This enables the unit to accept data or other information from an active talker on the loop.

5. Unlisten (UNL). This message is sent by the controller and causes all devices currently addressed as listeners to go into an inactive state.

6. Talk Address (TAD). This command is sent to one device on the loop to cause it to become a talker. There can be only one active talker on the loop at any given time.

7. Untalk (UNT). This command causes the currently addressed talker on the loop to become inactive.

HP-IL MESSAGE TABLE

Table 9-1 is a listing of the messages specified for HP-IL. In this listing, A is an address bit and X is a "don't care" bit. For Parallel Poll Enable the decimal value of BBB bits assign a service request bit D0 through D7. S is the sense bit which is 1 when a device needs service and 0 when it does not.

Table 9-1. HP-IL message table.

NAME	MESSAGE CODING	CLASS	MESSAGE FUNCTION	SUB GROUP
AAD	101 100 AAAAA	Ready	Auto Address 0–30	AAG
AAG	101 100 XXXXX	Ready	Auto Address Group	—
AAU	100 1001 1010	Command	Auto Address Unconfigure	UCG
ACG•	100 X000 XXXX	Command	Addressed Command Group	—
AEP	101 101 AAAAA	Ready	Auto Extended Primary	AAG
AES	101 110 AAAAA	Ready	Auto Extended Secondary	AAG
AMP	101 111 AAAAA	Ready	Auto Multiple Primary	AAG
ARG	101 01XX XXXX	Ready	Addressed Ready Group	—
CMD	100 XXXX XXXX	Command	Command Class Message	—
DAB	00X XXXX XXXX	Data or End	Data Byte	—
DCL	100 0001 0100	Command	Device Clear	UCG
DDL	100 101X XXXX	Command	Device Dependent Listener	ACG
DDT	100 110X XXXX	Command	Device Dependent Talker	ACG
DOE	0XX XXXX XXXX	Data or End	Data or End Class	—
EAR	100 0001 1000	Command	Enable Asynchronous Requests	UCG
END	01X XXXX XXXX	Data or End	End Byte	—
EOT	101 0100 000X	Ready	End of Transmission	ARG
ETE	101 0100 0001	Ready	End of Transmission – Error	ARG
ETO	101 0100 0000	Ready	End of Transmission – OK	ARG
GET	100 0000 1000	Command	Group Execute Trigger	ACG
GTL	100 0000 0001	Command	Go to Local	ACG
IAA	101 100 1111	Ready	Illegal Auto Address	AAG
IDY	11X XXXX XXXX	Identify	Identify	—
IEP	101 101 1111	Ready	Illegal Extended Primary	AAG
IES	101 110 1111	Ready	Illegal Extended Secondary	AAG
IFC	100 1001 0000	Command	Interface Clear	UCG
IMP	101 111 1111	Ready	Illegal Multiple Primary	AAG
LAD	100 001 AAAA	Command	Listen Address (0–30)	LAG
LAG	100 001X XXXX	Command	Listen Address Group	—
LLO	100 0001 0001	Command	Local Lockout	UCG
LPD	100 1001 1011	Command	Loop Power Down	UCG
MLA	100 001 AAAAA	Command	My Listen Address	LAG
MSA	100 011 AAAAA	Command	My Secondary Address	SAG
MTA	100 010 AAAAA	Command	My Talk Address	TAG
NAA	101 100 AAAAA	Ready	Next Auto Address	AAG
NES	101 110 AAAAA	Ready	Next Extended Secondary	AAG
NMP	101 111 AAAAA	Ready	Next Multiple Primary	AAG
NRD	101 0100 0010	Ready	Not Ready for Data	ARG
NRE	100 1001 0011	Command	Not Remote Enable	UCG
NUL	100 0000 0000	Command	Null Command	ACG
OSA	100 011 AAAAA	Command	Other Secondary Address	SAG
OTA	100 010 AAAAA	Command	Orher Talk Address	TAG
PPD	100 0000 0101	Command	Parallel Poll Disable	ACG
PPE	100 1000 SBBB	Command	Parallel Poll Enable	ACG
PPU	100 0001 0101	Command	Parallel Poll Unconfigure	UCG
RDY	101 XXXX XXXX	Ready	Ready Class	—
REN	100 1001 0010	Commmand	Remote Enable	UCG
RFC	101 0000 0000	Ready	Ready for Command	—
SAD	100 011 AAAAA	Command	Secondary Address	SAG
SAG	100 011X XXXX	Command	Secondary Address Group	—
SAI	101 0110 0011	Ready	Send Accessory ID	ARG
SDA	101 0110 0000	Ready	Send Data	ARG
SDC	100 0000 0100	Command	Selected Device Clear	ACG
SDI	101 0110 0010	Ready	Send Device ID	ARG
SOT	101 0110 0XXX	Ready	Start of Transmission	ARG
SRQ••	0X1 XXXX XXXX	DOE or IDY	Service Request	—
SST	101 0110 0001	Ready	Send Status	ARG
TAD	100 010 AAAAA	Command	Talk Address	TAG
TAG	100 010X XXXX	Command	Talk Address Group	—
TCT	101 0110 0100	Ready	Take Control	ARG
UCG	100 X001 XXXX	Command	Universal Command Group	—
UNL	100 0011 1111	Command	Unlisten	LAG
UNT	100 0101 1111	Command	Untalk	TAG
ZES	101 110 0000	Ready	Zero Extended Secondary	AAG

Chapter 10

Increasing GPIB System Performance

OVERVIEW

This chapter will explore some of the ways in which an automatic GPIB test system can be improved to take full advantage of the capability of IEEE-488. When the software for an automatic test system using the IEEE-488 interface has been debugged and is running in accordance with the requirements of the required tests, it probably can be improved through the use of techniques which have been designed into many GPIB controllers and instruments for maximum performance. Just as any operating computer program can be improved with a second look, so can the IEEE-488.

Probably one of the most important considerations in designing a GPIB system for maximum performance is the choice of the instruments to be used in the system. Because there is such a vast selection of controllers, personal and larger computers, and GPIB devices available today, the selection of the best instruments for the job can be difficult. Of course, in many cases it is necessary to use whatever hardware is on hand, but it may be possible to justify a capital expenditure to improve the operation, accuracy, and speed of a test system.

It is important for the software engineer to be familiar with the capabilities of the controller and every instrument or device he or she plans to use. Such familiarity will always result in a better program sequence and more efficient use of valuable time during the automatic test sequence. For example, a digital meter can be programmed to operate on a designated range or can be allowed to seek its own range through its autoranging feature. In any test setup, it is almost always better to specify the required instrument range rather than have it search through all ranges until the best one is obtained. It is very obvious that much test time can be lost while a digital voltmeter takes multiple readings while its autoranging circuits settle down to the proper range.

Another important consideration which can provide the most efficient GPIB test system is the choice of the controller, which may be an common PC, a sophisticated high-performance work station, or anything in between. If the automatic test system is essentially self-contained and requires very little interaction from an operator, almost any type of GPIB controller will do the job. Using a more elaborate type of unit will not be cost effective in the amount of time which can be saved. When much human interaction is required, it makes good sense to investigate the latest technology which has been developed to make the IEEE-488 system more understandable and easier to use.

A controller such as the Fluke 1722A has been designed to be well-suited to applications in which semiskilled personnel need to operate complex systems which perform sophisticated tests and measurements. A friendly graphics display has replaced the often intimidating keyboard, and the operator is prompted one step at a time. Response to the prompts is accomplished by touching the screen at the appropriate point. Such a system can always be updated as new software becomes available.

It is not necessary for the software engineer to have intimate knowledge of the controller and instrument programming codes and data formats. Software vendors have developed PC-based software development tools which include libraries of many popular IEEE-488 instruments. These tools provide on-screen descriptions (including graphics) of the instruments functions. The software automatically assembles the programming string to transmit the message to the IEEE-488 bus. For those GPIB instruments which are not a part of the software library, it is always possible to write the required programming, although this may be a difficult task.

INSTRUMENT SETUP TIME

Instrument setup time is composed of two parts: the time required for the device to accept and decode a command and the time required for that command to be fulfilled. The former represents a very small part of the time required for the sequence to be completed. It is the second part, called settling time, where the software engineer should concentrate his or her efforts to maximize system performance.

To help reduce setup time in the GPIB system, the number of setting changes in the program should be kept to a minimum. Wherever possible, command the instruments to the desired settings early in the program before the actual functions are needed. A good example of this is in the programming of a power supply. To avoid the relatively long settling time between the command and the actual desired voltage output, the power supply should be set up before it is needed, making WAIT statements in the program unnecessary. If the default mode of an instrument is satisfactory, use it since there will then be no need for a programming step to set that instrument up. If several tests are required which use the same instrument settings, group these tests in the program.

If any instrument on the bus provides internal setting storage, take advantage of it. This will help minimize setup time by reducing the time required to transfer and process the setting commands. An example of such an instrument is the Tektronix FG 5010 function generator, which can store 10 instrument setups. Bear in mind that storage of instrument settings does not reduce the settling time required by the device.

Software techniques can often help improve system speed. If the settling time of an instrument is known, a simple WAIT statement in the program can be used to halt the program sequence. Another method is to take several readings in rapid succession and compare them. When the readings are within a fixed desired window, they can be considered valid.

Be familiar with the operational aspects of the instruments on the bus. Some newer devices have a fast handshake and other features (program storage, buffering, etc.) built-in. Allow "smart" GPIB instruments to perform time-consuming tasks through hardware features which otherwise may require many lines of software programming.

Wherever possible, avoid unnecessary unaddressing and read-dressing steps. Bear in mind that when any device is addressed, all others automatically become unaddressed. Suppress unneeded terminators, and use GPIB commands instead of device-dependent commands if possible. Suppress leading and trailing spaces. For example, the HP-IB BASIC command, OUTPUT 701; A$, will transmit 19 spaces after A$ and before the CR/LF. A faster command would be OUTPUT 701 USING "K"; A$, which sends out no spaces.

Refer to the operating manual of the instruments that are being used on the bus to determine if response time can be improved by turning off certain functions when not needed. For example, blanking an instrument display or CRT can save programming time since the instrument is not required to update the display whenever it receives new data. The same holds true for other functions, such as autozeroing. If the feature is not required for the test, delete it using the device-dependent message from the controller.

One of the best methods to improve system performance is through the specialists and system engineers of the manufacturers of the GPIB equipment and hardware that is being used. Through their intimate knowledge of the instrumentation they can usually provide timely answers to questions regarding the improvement of system speed and performance.

DATA ACQUISITION

There are two major areas of data acquisition time which must be considered in the IEEE-488 interface system. These are trigger delay and digitizing time.

Trigger delay occurs when a software command or external event directs a GPIB instrument (such as a voltmeter) to begin accumulating data. It is the time between the point when the instrument is ready to accumulate data and the point when the trigger actually occurs. This is illustrated in Figure 10-1. If the instrument is busy capturing pretrigger data when the trigger is initiated, it will ignore that trigger until a new cycle of data acquisition is completed. Included in the trigger delay time is hold-off time, if the GPIB instrument is designed or programmed for that parameter.

The second part of data acquisition time of an instrument is called digitizing time. This is the time required for the device to perform the sampling of the measured data, digitize, and latch it so that it can be transmitted on the bus. The conversion time of a common analog-to-digital converter is a good example of digitizing time, which can be calculated as the reciprocal of the conversion rate. The 1/3-second reading rate of many digital voltmeters is a good example of digitizing time, which may be as much as 300 milliseconds.

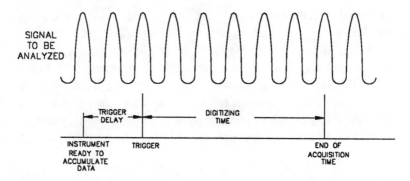

Figure 10-1.   Trigger delay and data acquisition time.

Many smart GPIB instruments provide the software engineer with some latitude in the amount of digitizing time that will be required in the program. For example, the Fluke 8840A digital voltmeter allows the measurement rate to be front panel or GPIB selected as 2.5, 20, or 100 readings per second. Of course, one does not get something for nothing; when the faster rates are chosen, there must be some sacrifice in measurement resolution and accuracy.

It is important to consider the operating options which are available to the software engineer when programming a device to acquire data. For example, a digital voltmeter will self-trigger (free run) at a predetermined rate. When the program directs the meter to send out a reading, the meter may be able to transmit to the bus the latest reading if it is stored in a buffer. Another method would be to hold the meter in standby mode until the TRIGGER command is received from the controller. This will initiate a conversion cycle which then can transmit data to the bus by means of the TALK command. The choice of which method to use for the best operating speed of the system depends upon the application and hardware available.

DATA TRANSFER

In order for the interface system to be useful, it is usually necessary for measurement or other data to be transferred over the bus from one instrument to another, and this part of the communication sequence can take a large part of the time required to accomplish the necessary tests. Data transfer time is defined as the time required for one device to transfer data to another. This will depend upon the number of data bytes that are to be transferred and the data transfer rate.

The IEEE-488 document specifies a maximum data rate of 250 kilobytes per second over a distance of 20 meters with one device every 2 meters of cable using open collector drivers. This rate can be 500 kilobytes per second if the drivers are designed with tri-state outputs (interface capability E2).

The data transfer rate can be further increased by restricting the system to certain requirements. Up to 1 megabyte per second can be achieved if the cable length is limited to 15 meters total length with one device connected every meter, and the maximum capacitance of each device on each line is 50-picofarads capacitance (except REN and IFC). All high-rate talkers should use a minimum multiline message settling time (T1 interface capability) of 350 nanoseconds. Buffered data byte storage in the devices provides additional advantages.

Although the data transfer rate for GPIP devices is usually specified by the manufacturer, the actual rate when operating in a real system with other GPIB instruments and devices will depend on a number of factors and will most certainly be less. Because the IEEE-488 system is asynchronous, any data transfer must take place at a rate which is determined by the slowest addressed receptor. When one such device is much slower than all others, the data transfer rate will be approximately equal to that device's rate. Because of this, it would not be possible to improve the data transfer rate by using faster instruments on the bus unless the speed of the slowest unit is addressed first.

Precision measurements typically take the greatest portion of the time when compared to the microsecond response times in modern desktop and minicomputers. Five and one-half digit voltage measurements using standard analog-to-digital techniques, narrow band spectrum analysis, and precision low-frequency counting are examples of slow real-time measurement processes. Smart instruments and peripherals can provide easier and faster digital signal processing such as high-speed sampling, burst measurements, and block memory transfers. These techniques will create increased demands on the GPIB system.

One method to achieve increased performance with high-speed talkers is by operating the instrument in talk-only function and opening up a direct memory access (DMA) channel to transfer the data directly into the controller's memory. The talker should be operated in its automatic retriggering mode so that a new measurement is initiated as soon as it has finished the previous one. With such fast data transfer the instrument must be able to send the readings over the IEEE-488 bus within the time it takes to generate a new set of data. To ensure that the bus gets instant access to the controller's memory, its processor may have to be temporarily halted while the fast I/O sequence takes place, and a mechanism must be implemented in the software to return control to the program when the DMA buffer is full.

Some IEEE-488 controllers have more than one port, and one may be faster than the other. The Tektronix 4041 system controller, for example, provides a optional high-speed port which is capable of data transfers using direct memory access. The higher-speed instruments and those which transfer the most data should be placed on the faster port. Slower instruments, if they are not involved with most data transfers, do not need to be placed on a different bus.

If two or more instruments regularly send data to each other, avoid separating them. It may be possible to have such units addressed to communicate with each other without involving the controller. It would be poor practice to place two instruments which transfer data between them on different buses. To do so would use up much valuable time as the data would have to pass through the controller as it is transferred from one bus to the other.

When it is necessary to transmit large amounts of data over the bus, it would be more efficient to use the binary code instead of ASCII, which in a typical system may provide 2 to 1 or greater reduction in the number of bytes that would be required. An ASCII number requires 1 byte for each digit, while the same byte can be used to transmit a far larger number in binary. The number 255 would require 3 bytes if coded in ASCII, but a single byte in binary (11111111) could be used to transmit the same number. When more than 1 byte is used to transmit data in binary, the difference becomes astronomical. Three bytes coded in binary can be used to transmit the number 16,777,225. That's equivalent to 8 ASCII bytes.

The Tektronix Codes and Formats document calls out a specific "binary block argument" which must be used when transferring data in binary. This is illustrated in Figure 10-2. The binary block argument must begin with the percent character, %, followed by a set of bytes. Immediately following the % character is a 2-byte field which is a 16-bit binary integer that specifies the number of data bytes to follow. A final byte contains an 8-bit checksum to allow the listener to verify that the data contained within the binary integer and binary data bytes is valid. It would be prudent to program the listener to calculate the checksum of the binary block transfer to ensure that the message received was correct.

When using the binary block transfer, it is important to use the EOI terminator at the end of the message to avoid the possibility that a binary block data transmission could coincidentally contain

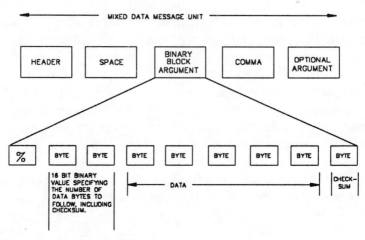

Figure 10-2.   Structure of binary block argument.

the ASCII CR/LF character. A listener programmed to respond to such a terminator would stop listening in the middle of the transmission and the binary data would be lost.

DATA PROCESSING

Data processing time is a significant factor in GPIB performance, and it will depend on not only the hardware used, but the method by which the data is processed by the commands of the software. A large part of the time required for this task is a function of the speed of the controller; it makes good sense to choose one which is compatible with the desired time that can be devoted to processing. A simple way to measure data processing time is to run a sample program and allow the controller to measure the time required by means of its built-in real time clock. This easily implemented method can be very valuable comparing one software program or one controller with another.

It is often possible to allow smart instruments on the bus to share the burden of data processing. For example, it would be faster to send a measurement result to the controller rather than transmitting a large number of data bytes which must be processed by the controller. While the instruments on the bus are being used in this way, it will be possible for the controller to concentrate on the next task at hand. In effect, there would be two or more instruments in the system processing data at the same time.

If the system allows queuing of processing tasks, this can be used to further increase system performance. By stacking these tasks, it becomes possible to perform them at a time when it is convenient for the controller or instrument to handle.

THE HUMAN INTERFACE

Since the IEEE-488 interface bus was first available to provide the capability of automatic test systems, it has improved steadily with dramatic speed over its relatively short life. Today there are literally thousands of instruments available, and a vast selection of controllers, hardware, and software to make it possible to design almost any test setup imagined. But the most sophisticated system is no better than the human technician or operator which must make it work. Human interaction is by and large the weakest link in any automatic test setup.

It is the job of the software engineer to ensure that any possible ambiguity or communication problem with the test technician is designed out of the system. Admittedly, this is much easier to say than do. But the tools to accomplish this are readily at hand, in the form of a computer display CRT, keyboard, touch screen, and mouse.

One of the most difficult parts of writing a test sequence which a totally unfamiliar operator must use is to make the instructions clear enough so that no possible misinterpretation can be made. It is all too easy to skip over an obvious point only to find that the technician who must follow the instructions is totally confused. One way to eliminate most of these problems is to have a "dress rehearsal" of the test sequence with a technician who is totally unfamiliar with the instruments or system. This method can be quite successful, but it may require several revisions of the original test program before the engineer is satisfied that it has been made as foolproof as possible.

The display CRT can be used very effectively to state the exact instructions which must be followed. The software engineer must anticipate any possible error or incorrect action by the operator and prevent any possible damage or loss of valuable test time in the event that a wrong key is pressed or an instrument is not properly connected or adjusted. It is always best to lead the operator through the test sequence, one step at a time using prompts, rather than assume that he or she can perform a multistep operation no matter how simple it may be. Simple graphics or screen menus can be very valuable tools to accomplish this.

As one gathers experience writing test programs, soon each succeeding program will be more elegant and troublefree than the previous one. We learn from our mistakes, and this seems to confirm the saying that experience is the best teacher.

Chapter 11

Case Histories and Applications of the IEEE-488 Bus System

Although one may be very knowledgeable about the information presented in the preceding chapters of this book, there is no substitute for an actual hands-on exercise of a real world application of the IEEE-488 Interface System to appreciate its vast potential. The purpose of this section is to share with you some very real applications of automatic test systems and to show how some of these problems were solved using GPIB components. While the following test setups and ATE programming sequences may not be representative of your particular application, it is hoped that they will provide you with some insight as to how to design test positions and write software for an IEEE-488 automatic test station and enhance the automatic testing of your product.

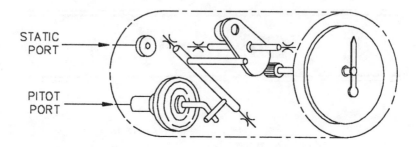

STATIC
PORT

PITOT
PORT

Figure 11-1.   Simplified diagram of airspeed indicator showing capsule and mechanical linkage to pointer.

AIRSPEED CAPSULE DISPLACEMENT

Pneumatic airspeed indicators, as used in all kinds of aircraft, contain some kind of pressure transducer which exhibits a mechanical displacement in response to air pressure. These transducers are commonly referred to as capsules. An airspeed indicator in an aircraft is driven by pressure that is developed by a pitot tube, which is simply a length of metal tubing which has an open end exposed to the relative wind. As the speed of the aircraft increases, the pressure developed by the pitot tube also increases. This relationship between airspeed and pressure permits the design of an airspeed indicator in which the displacement of the capsule, through a mechanical linkage and gear train, drives a pointer. A simplified illustration of this technique is illustrated in Figure 11-1. A pneumatic airspeed indicator, as opposed to an electronic device, has one important advantage: It will function properly in the event of a power failure in the aircraft.

Because we are dealing with aircraft instruments that have a direct bearing on human safety, airspeed indicators must have a certain guaranteed accuracy so that the pilot of the aircraft knows his or her airspeed at all times. As a result, the translation of pitot pressure to mechanical displacement in the transducer must be held to within very tight tolerances. This requires accurate instrumentation to measure capsule displacement versus air pressure.

Before sophisticated elecronic instrumentation came into being, the usual method of measuring airspeed capsule displacement was to provide a pressure/vacuum source, varied by a test technician in accordance with standard airspeed/pressure tables, to drive the capsule. Its expansion as a result of the pressure was measured with an accurate mechanical device such as a micrometer. The results were logged on a test data sheet and compared to the specification of the capsule. Accuracies of .001 inch and better were required.

This test sequence was time-consuming and could be subjected to error. The test technician could improperly set the pressure/vacuum source at a given check point or could make an error in the reading of the micrometer. Even worse, a tired technician could allow a transducer to pass the test, even though it did not meet accuracy specifications.

An automatic test station, operable without any form of human intervention (except to connect the unit under test and monitor the test sequence), solves this problem very nicely. Not only does the system provide accuracy equal to or better than the old method, it produces a hard copy of the test data and flags any unit that falls out of specification. Another advantage which cannot be overlooked is the improvement in speed. The automatic system can test airspeed capsules faster than a human.

To assemble an automatic displacement measuring system, the following state-of-the-art instruments were required:

1. An optical displacement detector which generates an analog voltage that is a linear function of the distance between its sensor and the capsule. Keyence model PA1830 Sensor and model PA1801 controller (Figure 11-2), manufactured by Keyence Corporation of America, Fair Lawn, New Jer-

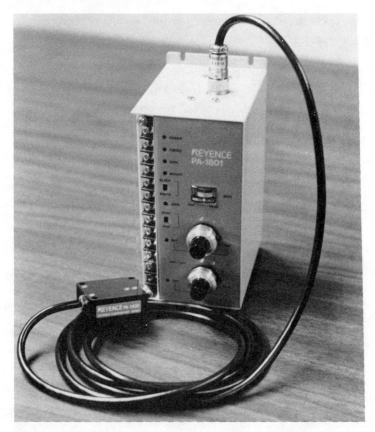

Figure 11-2.   Keyence optical displacement sensor. Courtesy of Keyence Corporation.

sey, was used. This instrument provides a displacement measurement range of ±5 millimeters (reference distance 40 millimeters) with an accuracy of 1 percent +5 micrometers. The sensor controller provides an output voltage of zero to ±5 volts at the maximum measurement distance of 5 millimeters.

2. A calibrated pressure/vacuum source which can be remotely controlled by means of an analog voltage. The Mensor model 12275 precision pressure controller, manufactured by Mensor Corporation, San Marcos, Texas, was used. This unit provides an accurate differential pressure, from 0 to 12 inches of mercury, when driven by a 0 to 5-volt dc power source. The controlled pressure, which is expressed in inches of mercury, is a linear function of the remote driving voltage.

3. A dc power source containing a digital to analog converter, to be accurately programmed through a GPIB digital I/O interface. The power supply containing the converter was constructed in-house, since commercial programmable supplies available at the time were not capable of resolving voltages to 1 millivolt, as required by the desired pressure accuracy. The digital I/O interface used was the Seitz model 6450P general-purpose parallel interface, equipped with the 64-bit I/O option, manufactured by Seitz Technical Products, Avondale, Pennsylvania.

In addition to the instruments described above a GPIB digital voltmeter, Fluke model 8840A, was used to measure the output of the Keyence optical displacement instrument. The controller in this test system was a Hewlett-Packard model HP85B computer. Figure 11-3 illustrates the test setup.

The capsule is tested in a sealed chamber by subjecting it to a differential pressure. Simulated pitot pressure is applied to the capsule-sensing orifice, and the ambient pressure within the chamber, called static pressure, is exposed to the low side of the pressure controller. This simulates the actual operating conditions of the capsule when it is sensing pitot pressure in the aircraft.

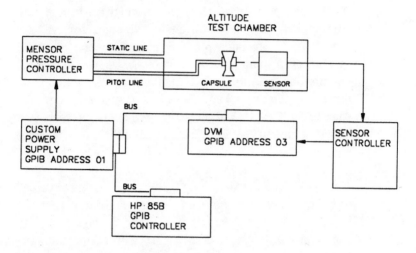

Figure 11-3.   Capsule displacement test setup.

The sensor assembly of the displacement instrument must also be placed in the same chamber, with a cable passing through to the outside to connect to its controller. A test fixture within the chamber provides the proper mechanical relationship between the capsule and optical detector, which is set to 40 millimeters when the capsule is at rest.

The automatic test sequence provides prompts in the computer display to properly lead the technician during the test, which checks capsule displacement at nine specified airspeed points from 0 to 350 knots. A graph containing the upper and lower test limits of the capsule, and the test results, is produced. A printout of the deviation from spec at each checkpoint is printed by the computer, including a second order calculation of the change in deviation from one checkpoint to the next.

Program 11-1 is the actual software which was used to perform the test sequence. In this application, the Seitz I/O interface was assigned an address of 01 and the Fluke DVM an address of 03.

```
10   ! CAPSULE TEST PROGRAM
20   DIM Q(9),R(9),Z1(9),Z2(9)
30   FOR X=0 TO 8
40   READ Q(X)
50   DATA 0,40,60,100,150,200,250,300,350
60   NEXT X
70   FOR X=0 TO 8
80   READ R(X)
90   DATA 0,.0049,.0106,.0274,.0519,.0746,.095,.1136,.1304
100  NEXT X
110  IMAGE 3D,4XD.DDDD,6X,D.DDDD
120  CLEAR
130  OUTPUT 703 ;"F1R3S0T0D0"
140  A1=29.92126
150  B1=518.67
160  C1=.00356616
170  D1=5.2559
180  B3=160.45478*10^-9
190  C3=6076.1135/3600
200  D3=3.5
210  DISP "THIS PROGRAM WILL CHECK AIRSPEED CAPSULE"
220  DISP "DISPLACEMENT FROM ZERO TO 350 KNOTS AIRSPEED"
230  DISP
240  DISP "SET MENSOR TO REMOTE CONTROL FUNCTION"
250  DISP
260  DISP "THEN PRESS CONTINUE KEY TO START THE TEST"
270  PAUSE
280  CLEAR
290  PRINT "A/S CAPSULE DISPLACEMENT TEST"
300  PRINT "FROM ZERO TO 350 KNOTS"
310  PRINT "A/S DEFLECTION ERROR"
320  PRINT
```

Program 11-1   *(continued)*

```
330 ENTER 703 ; V1
340 V1=INT (1000*V1+.5)/1000
350 FOR X=0 TO 8
360 P=A1*((1+B3*(Q(X)*C3)^2)^D3-1)
370 N=P*4095/3072
380 A2=INT (FP (N)*256)
390 B2=INT (N)
400 DISP Q(X);"KNOTS"
410 OUTPUT 701 USING "#,B" ; A2,B2
420 SEND 7 ; UNL
430 WAIT 5000
440 ENTER 703 ; V2
450 V2=INT (1000*V2+.5)/1000
460 Z=V2-V1
470 Z1(X)=Z*.03937
480 Z2(X)=INT (10000*Z1(X)+.5)/10000
490 PRINT USING 110 ; Q(X),-Z2(X),-Z2(X)-R(X)
500 NEXT X
510 PRINT
520 GCLEAR
530 PEN 1
540 SCALE 0,350,0,.15
550 XAXIS 0,50
560 YAXIS 0,.01
570 MOVE 85,.006
580 LABEL "100"
590 MOVE 185,.006
600 LABEL "200"
610 MOVE 285,.006
620 LABEL "300"
630 MOVE 9,.046
640 LABEL ".05"
```

Program 11-1   *(continued)*

```
650 MOVE 9,.096
660 LABEL ".10"
670 MOVE 9,.142
680 LABEL ".15"
690 MOVE 200,.02
700 LABEL "KNOTS"
710 MOVE 75,.142
720 LABEL "DISPL"
730 FOR X=0 TO 8
740 PLOT Q(X),1.1*R(X)
750 NEXT X
760 PEN UP
770 FOR X=0 TO 8
780 PLOT Q(X),.9*R(X)
790 NEXT X
800 PEN UP
810 FOR X=0 TO 8
820 PLOT Q(X),-Z2(X)
830 NEXT X
840   COPY
850 PRINT " A/S     DELTA 1   DELTA 2"
860 PRINT
870 PRINT USING 110 ; Q(1);,-Z2(1),-Z2(1)+Z2(0)
880 FOR X=2 TO 8
890 PRINT USING 110 ;Q(X),-Z2(X)+Z2(X-1),
                     -Z2(X)+2*Z2(X-1)-Z2(X-2)
900 NEXT X
910 CLEAR
920 DISP "TEST IS COMPLETED"
930 END
```

Program 11-1

The following explains the details of the capsule displacement test as implemented in Program 11-1:

Line 20 dimensions four variables which will be used in the calculations during the test.

Lines 30 through 60 assign airspeed checkpoint values to variable Q(X).

Lines 70 through 100 assign displacement specifications, in inches, to variable R(X).

Line 110 specifies a format for the test data report that will be printed by the computer.

Line 120 clears the computer display screen.

Line 130 programs the Fluke DVM to dc function, 20-volt range, slow reading rate, internal trigger mode, and normal display.

Lines 140 through 200 assign constants to variables which will be used in making calculations during the test.

Lines 210 through 260 provide a computer display to prompt the technician.

Line 270 halts the program, with the prompts displayed, so that the technician can set the Mensor pressure controller to the proper operating mode. When the technician is ready to resume the test sequence, the continue key is pressed.

Lines 290 through 320 direct the computer to print the heading of the test data form.

Line 330 directs the voltmeter to send a reading to the controller, which will store it in variable V1. This reading represents any possible offset voltage, produced by the displacement instrument, due to any position error in the test setup.

Line 340 rounds out the value stored in V1 to three decimal places.

Lines 350 through 500 are the complete test sequence which takes nine measurements, at nine different airspeeds (including zero) of capsule displacement. This is accomplished in a FOR-NEXT loop.

Line 360 calculates air pressure required for the selected airspeed of the test.

Lines 370 through 390 perform a mathematical calculation to produce two integers, A2 and B2. These integers are the numbers that will be required by the Seitz I/O interface to set a 12-bit word in its I/O output lines which are used to feed a 12-bit digital to analog converter in the programmable power supply. The result of this is that the supply will then generate the proper voltage to set the Mensor pressure controller to the airspeed represented by variable Q(X).

Line 400 displays the current airspeed being generated by the Mensor.

Line 410 directs the Seitz I/O interface to set the bits in its first 12 output lines in accordance with the calculations of lines 370 through 390.

Line 420 resets the Seitz I/O interface so that the next command to it will set the same I/O lines. This command is necessary because the Seitz unit has a total of 64 output lines and would normally respond to subsequent commands by setting the next 12 I/O lines.

Line 430 provides a 5-second waiting period for the pressure controller and capsule to stabilize before a displacement measurement is taken.

Line 440 directs the voltmeter to send its next reading to variable V2. This reading is the output voltage of the optical displacement instrument, and it represents the magnitude of expansion of the capsule due to the simulated airspeed pressure.

Line 450 rounds out V2 to three decimal places.

Line 460 calculates the net displacement of the capsule by subtracting the offset voltage measured in line 330.

Line 470 converts the capsule displacement from millimeters to inches, since the optical detector uses metric units of measure.

Line 480 rounds out the displacement measurement to four decimal places.

Line 490 directs the computer to print the current airspeed, displacement, and deviation from the displacement specification at this airspeed.

Lines 520 through 830 direct the computer to generate a graph of the complete test sequence, showing the actual performance of the capsule as well as the upper and lower limits of acceptable displacement. The graph, displayed on the controller's screen, provides an immediate visual indication of a pass or fail capsule. Figure 11-4 illustrates the CRT display.

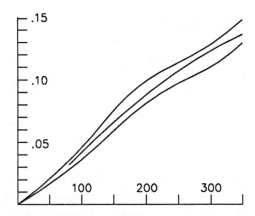

Figure 11-4.   Display of capsule test results.

Line 840 directs the computer to print a hard copy of the graph, for a permanent record of the test.

Lines 850 through 900 perform a calculation of deviation, called delta 1, and a second-order effect, called delta 2, which is the change in capsule error from one airspeed to the next. This parameter is used to diagnose any possible mechanical calibration errors in the capsule.

Line 920 informs the technician that the test has been completed so that the next capsule can be checked.

Figure 11-4 illustrates a typical graph of results which was printed by the computer. It shows the upper and lower limits of capsule displacement versus airspeed, as well as the actual capsule performance. This test data graph is a permanent record of the accuracy of the unit. Note that any capsule which did not meet specification is readily detected by means of the graph, which could provide the design engineer with valuable information to help correct the problem.

The above software program was essentially a first attempt to automate a production capsule displacement test. As with any computer program, a second look often can provide alternative methods, possibly more elegant, of performing the same test. Perhaps a revised program could produce greater accuracy or avoid a possible booby trap.

For example, let's look at line 430, which directs the test sequence to stop for 5 seconds while the pressure controller and capsule stabilize so that the measurement that follows represents a true reading of displacement. The time of 5 seconds was determined empirically; it seemed that the displacement sensor output became steady enough for a reading after this amount of time had passed. But suppose, in another test position, the time required was greater than 5 seconds? Here we have a possible situation which could produce disastrous results.

The solution to this problem is actually very simple, since we have a computer and automatic test station at our disposal which will rapidly perform any number of measurements and calculations. A better way to determine if a varying parameter has stabilized is to write a subroutine which continuously stores readings in alternate variables, such as V2 and V3. The routine monitors the difference between any two successive readings, and when it is within an acceptable limit, the latest reading is taken to be the final one. The program sequence can then return to the next step of the test.

Another improvement in the capsule test can be found in the printing of the test data form by the controller. If the test limits of the capsule were stored in additional variables, such as H(X) for the high limit and L(X) for the low limit, the computer could perform a "greater than" or "less than" comparison and print directly on the test data form a pass or fail notation. The level of sophistication of any automatic test sequence is limited only by your imagination.

As you can see, this very involved test sequence of a pneumatic airspeed capsule has been performed by a simple test program, using a relatively small number of instruments and hardware. A calculation of the amount of technician time that could be saved in a production run of hundreds or thousands of capsules would show that the payback time of the cost of instrumentation would be very short.

SERVO ALTIMETER RATE MEASUREMENT

This application of the GPIB system was brought about through a unique test situation which could not be satisfactorily solved by ordinary test methods. In the case of servo altimeter rate measurement, it was not possible for the technician to make a realistic, repeatable measurement; it required the objectivity and power of a computer. Here is a perfect example of how an automatic GPIB test system provided an answer to an unusual production test problem.

A servo altimeter is an aircraft instrument which provides a reading of altitude by means of a motor driven gear train and pointer. The advantage of such an instrument is that the motor is capable of driving, at a fast rate of speed, not only the pointer mechanism but other mechanical components as well. A purely pneumatic capsule driven altimeter cannot perform such a function since the load on the capsule must be held to an absolute minimum for accurate altitude readings.

One of the components that a servo altimeter may contain is a tachometer, which is actually a small generator that produces an output voltage which is a function of its shaft speed, or rpm. The tachometer is mechanically coupled to the altimeter gear train so that the rate of climb or rate of descent of the aircraft can be translated into a voltage. This voltage, called rate output, is one of the test parameters of the servo altimeter, and it was made at a constant rate of climb or descent of 4000 feet per minute.

The particular test setup in which a seemingly impossible accurate rate measurement had to be made involved a line of servo altimeters which exhibited a certain amount of gear train jitter. This was inherent in the design of the mechanics of the servo unit, and there was no way to eliminate it. Since the specifications for the rate output required an average measurement with an accuracy of ±5 percent, the test equipment included various forms of long time-constant filters which removed the jitter in the rate voltage reading and produced an average output. Without using any form of filtering, a digital meter could easily measure instantaneous voltage excursions of 20 percent or more from the average rate output value.

This system of rate measurement was mediocre at best; units that were passed by test technicians were rejected by quality control personnel. Part of the problem was the subjectivity of the measurement, which varied as the altimeter was exercised through a large range of altitude. After making several attempts to find ways to avoid QC rejects, it became apparent that the human element of this test had to be eliminated. This was a natural for an automatic test system using GPIB components.

It was decided that a large number of instantaneous rate output voltage measurements would be taken over a specified change in altitude, both ascending and descending. Each voltage reading would be stored in the controller's memory, and the calculated average would be printed out on a test data form as the measured rate output of the unit. As the measurements were being assimilated by the computer, a graph of rate output versus altitude was reproduced on the CRT. Since this technique does not depend upon any human interpretation of meter readings, the results of the test were remarkably repeatable regardless of which person ran the test. QC rejections were virtually eliminated. An additional benefit of this technique of rate measurement, totally unexpected, was in the

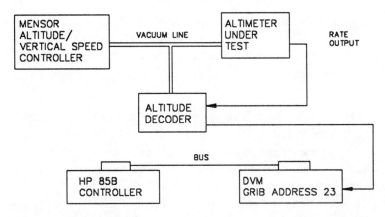

Figure 11-5.   Servo altimeter rate test setup.

graph reproduced on the controller CRT and test data form. A trained technician could analyze the performance of rejected units and often determine the cause of failure.

Figure 11-5 illustrates the test setup for the servo altimeter rate measurement. The controller for the test sequence was the HP 85B computer. This automatic test station required the following instrumentation which was readily available, except for an altitude decoding instrument, designed and constructed in house:

1. Hewlett-Packard 3478A digital voltmeter; set to GPIB address 23.
2. Mensor altitude/vertical speed test set, model 10620, to provide a constant rate of change in simulated altitude as required by the test.
3. Custom designed interface unit which contains logic circuitry to detect specific altitude levels. This was accomplished by monitoring a built-in test altimeter containing a transponder mode C altitude reporting encoder

and decoding the altitude reporting digital output word of the altimeter. The GPIB voltmeter was used to inform the controller of the crossover of the chosen altitude points of the test.

The technician performing the test sequence was directed by prompts on the controller display CRT to set the manually operated altitude test set to the required altitudes and rate of climb or descent. Once this was done, the automatic test sequence took over and ran the complete climb and descent without the need for any human interaction. The test sequence, provided by the software, consists of the following steps:

1. The technician is instructed to enter via the keyboard pertinent data which will be printed on the test data produced by the computer.
2. The technician is instructed to raise the simulated altitude to 18000 feet, set the climb rate to 4000 feet per minute, and start the automatic test sequence.
3. The computer generates a graph on the display CRT which provides a visual readout of the measurements of rate voltage as they are being taken. This enables the technician to abort the test if it is obvious that the rate measurement is out of spec.
4. The automatic test sequence instructs the voltmeter to take 100 instantaneous measurements of rate output over an altitude change of 4000 feet (1 minute of time), and stores them in computer memory.
5. When the climb test is completed, the program pauses so that the resulting graph display can be assimilated by the technician. The computed average rate measurement is printed on the test data form.

6. The technician is directed to start the descend test by raising the simulated altitude to 28,000 feet, set the descend rate to 4000 feet per minute, and start the automatic sequence.

7. The computer takes control of the test and, as done previously in the climb test, a graph of results is plotted as the measurements are being taken. The technician can abort the test if the results are obviously out of spec.

8. When the 100 measurements are completed over a period of 1 minute, the computer prints the calculated average on the test data form. The graph remains on the display CRT until the technician manually causes the sequence to resume by pressing the continue key.

9. The computer analyzes the test results and prints pass or fail for each of the two parts of the test.

Program 11-2, which follows, is the actual program which was used in the servo altimeter rate measurement sequence.

The following will serve to explain the pertinent steps of Program 11-2:

Line 30 sets aside sections of computer memory which will store the climb and descend rate measurements.

Lines 40 through 290 provide display prompts on the screen of the computer to instruct the technician in the proper administration of the test and prints on the test data form the identification of the unit under test as well as the name of the tester.

Lines 310 through 520 instruct the computer to prepare a graph display with the desired coordinates and scale factors.

Line 530 sets the operating functions and range scale of the voltmeter.

```
10    CLEAR
20    DIM A$[20]
30    DIM A(100).B(100)
40    DISP "THIS PROGRAM WILL CHECK RATE OUTPUT"
50    DISP "FOLLOW INSTRUCTIONS AS DISPLAYED HERE"
60    DISP "PRESS CONTINUE KEY TO START TEST"
70    PAUSE
80    CLEAR
90    DISP "TYPE UNIT SERIAL NUMBER, YOUR NAME, AND"
100 DISP "TODAY'S DATE SEPARATED BY COMMAS."
105 DISP "THEN PRESS END LINE KEY."
110 INPUT A$,B$,C$
120 CLEAR
130 PRINT A$;" RATE TEST"
140 PRINT "DATED ";C$;" BY ";B$
150 ON KEY# 1,"CLIMB" GOSUB 1440
160 ON KEY# 2,"DESCEND" GOSUB 1490
170 DISP "NOTE: TO RESTART THE CLIMB TEST PRESS KEY K1"
180 DISP "      TO RESTART THE DESCEND TEST PRESS KEY K2"
190 DISP "RAISE ALTIMETER TO 18000 FEET"
200 DISP "THEN PRESS CONTINUE KEY"
210 KEY LABEL
220 PAUSE
230 CLEAR
240 DISP "WHEN THE CLIMB TEST IS COMPLETED THE"
250 DISP "COMPUTER WILL SOUND."
260 DISP "AT THAT TIME PRESS CONTINUE KEY"
270 DISP "TO START THE DESCEND TEST"
280 DISP "SET MENSOR TO CLIMB AT 4000 FEET/MINUTE"
290 DISP "THEN PRESS CONTINUE KEY"
300 PAUSE
```

Program 11-2   *(continued)*

```
310 PEN UP
320 GCLEAR
330 SCALE 1,100,.9,1.1
340 XAXIS 1,12.5
350 YAXIS 1,.01
360 MOVE 2,.9
370 LABEL ".9"
380 MOVE 2,.945
390 LABEL ".95"
400 MOVE 2,1.045
410 LABEL "1.05"
420 MOVE 2,1.094
430 LABEL "1.1"
440 MOVE 22,.99
450 LABEL "21K"
460 MOVE 48,.99
470 LABEL "22K"
480 MOVE 73,.99
490 LABEL "23K"
500 MOVE 16,1.09
510 LABEL "CLIMB RATE VOLTAGE OUTPUT"
520 PEN UP
530 OUTPUT 723 ;"F2R1N40T1D1"
540 ENTER 723 ; V
550 IF V<4 THEN 560 ELSE 540
560 TO=TIME
570 WAIT 19000
580 FOR X=1 TO 100
590 ENTER 723 ; A(X)
600 PLOT X,A(X)
610 WAIT 28
620 NEXT X
```

Program 11-2   *(continued)*

```
630 WAIT 5000
640 ENTER 723 ; V
650 IF V>2 THEN 660 ELSE 640
660 T1=TIME
670 PRINT "MENSOR TIME = ";T1-T0
680 GOSUB 1540
690 PAUSE
700 C=0
710 FOR X=1 TO 100
720 C=C+A(X)
730 NEXT X
740 DISP "CLIMB RATE OUTPUT = ";INT (1000*C/100+.5)/1000
750 PRINT "CLIMB RATE - ";INT (1000*C/100+.5)/1000
760 DISP "PRESS CONTINUE KEY TO START DESCEND TEST"
770 PAUSE
780 CLEAR
790 DISP "RAISE ALTITUDE TO 28000 FEET,"
800 DISP "THEN PRESS CONTINUE KEY"
810 PAUSE
820 CLEAR
830 DISP "WHEN DESCEND TEST IS COMPLETED"
840 DISP "THE COMPUTER WILL SOUND."
850 DISP "PRESS CONTINUE KEY AT THAT TIME"
860 DISP "TO COMPLETE THE TEST"
870 DISP "TO START DESCEND TEST"
880 DISP "SET MENSOR TO DESCEND AT 4000 FEET/MINUTE"
890 DISP "THEN PRESS CONTINUE KEY"
900 PAUSE
910 PEN UP
920 GCLEAR
930 SCALE 1,100,.9,1.1
```

Program 11-2   *(continued)*

```
940 XAXIS 1,12.5
950 YAXIS 1,.01
960 MOVE 2,.9
970 LABEL ".9"
980 MOVE 2,.945
990 LABEL ".95"
1000 MOVE 2,1.045
1010 LABEL "1.05"
1020 MOVE 2,1.094
1030 LABEL "1.1"
1040 MOVE 22,.99
1050 LABEL "23K"
1060 MOVE 48,.99
1070 LABEL "22K"
1080 MOVE 73,.99
1090 LABEL "21K"
1100 MOVE 16,1.09
1110 LABEL "DESCEND RATE VOLTAGE OUTPUT"
1120 PEN UP
1130 OUTPUT 723 ;"F2R1N4Z0T1D1"
1140 ENTER 723 ; V
1150 IF V<4 THEN 1160 ELSE 1140
1160 TO=TIME
1170 WAIT 19000
1180 FOR X=1 TO 100
1190 ENTER 723 ; B(X)
1200 PLOT X,B(X)
1210 WAIT 28
1220 NEXT X 1230 WAIT 5000
1240 ENTER 723 ; V
1250 IF V>2 THEN 1260 ELSE 1240
```

Program 11-2   *(continued)*

```
1260 T1=TIME
1270 PRINT "MENSOR TIME =";T1-T0
1280 GOSUB 1540
1290 PAUSE
1300 D=0
1310 FOR X=1 TO 100
1320 D=D+B(X)
1330 NEXT X
1340 DISP "DESCEND RATE OUTPUT = ";INT
(1000*D/100+.5)/1000
1350 PRINT "DESCEND RATE - ";INT (1000*D/100+.5)/1000
1360 IF C/100>1.05 OR C100<.95 THEN 1370 ELSE 1380
1370 PRINT "ALTIMETER FAILED CLIMB TEST" @ GOTO 1390
1380 PRINT "ALTIMETER PASSED CLIMB TEST"
1390 IF D/100>1.05 OR D/100<.95 THEN 1400 ELSE 1420
1400 PRINT "ALTIMETER FAILED DESCEND TEST"
1410 END
1420 PRINT "ALTIMETER PASSED DESCEND TEST"
1430 END
1440 CLEAR
1450 DISP "RETURN ALTIMETER TO 18000 FEET"
1460 DISP "THEN PRESS CONTINUE KEY"
1470 PAUSE
1480 GOTO 230
1490 CLEAR
1500 DISP "RETURN ALTIMETER TO 28000 FEET"
1510 DISP "THEN PRESS CONTINUE KEY"
1520 PAUSE
1530 GOTO 820
1540 FOR X=1 TO 10
1550 BEEP 130,100
```

Program 11-2   *(continued)*

```
1560 WAIT 20
1570 NEXT X
1580 RETURN
```

Program 11-2

Lines 540 and 550 form a recycling loop which halts the program sequence until the altitude of the vacuum/pressure simulator reaches 19,000 feet. This is accomplished through the logic circuits of the in-house test unit which decodes the output of its built-in altitude reporting encoder.

Line 560 provides a time reference for the start of the automatic sequence, to measure the elapsed time which will be a 2-minute interval during the 19K to 27K change in simulated altitude at a climb rate of 4000 feet per minute.

Line 570 provides a 19-second delay in the program to allow the altimeter to reach an altitude of about 20,000 feet. The actual altitude at the start of the rate measurement sequence is not a significant parameter in this test.

Lines 580 through 620 form a FOR-NEXT loop which instructs the voltmeter to take 100 rate measurements to be stored in variable A(X). The measurements are spaced out by 28 milliseconds (to provide 1 minute of measuring time) and each rate measurement is plotted on the computer screen as it is assimilated by the controller.

Lines 640 and 650 form a recycling loop which halts the program until the decoded output of the altitude encoder informs the computer that an altitude of 27,000 feet has been reached.

Lines 660 and 670 allow the computer to calculate the time interval required for the altitude simulator to cover the 19K to 27K altitude change. The result is printed on the test data form and serves as a check of altitude simulater climb rate accuracy.

Line 680 is a subprogram which causes the computer to sound and alert the technician that the climb test has been completed.

Lines 700 through 730 instruct the computer to add and store the set of 100 rate measurement readings.

Lines 740 through 890 print the climb rate results on the test data form and provide display prompts to the technician.

Lines 910 through 1360 provide the descend sequence, similar to that described above for the climb test.

Lines 1370 through 1430 instruct the computer to print the appropriate pass or fail flags on the test data form.

Lines 1440 through 1530 contain two subprograms which are executed when the technician aborts the climb or descend test by means of the user defined keys K1 and K2.

Figure 11-6 illustrates the resulting graph which is reproduced on the computer CRT and test data sheet. Note the variation of instantaneous rate measurements, as recorded by the computer. Since the aircraft navigation system responds to only the average rate output of the altimeter, the computed results of the test represent a meaningful rate output measurement.

Note that a custom designed interface unit as illustrated in Figure 11-6 would not be necessary in a test setup such as this if a GPIB programmable altitude test set was available at the time. One such test test set is available from Kollsman Instrument Company,

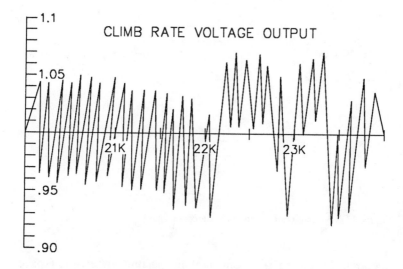

Figure 11-6.   Graph of climb rate measurement.

Merrimack, New Hampshire. This fully programmable test set can be programmed to simulate any altitude and vertical speed within the capabilities of the instrument, greatly simplifying the automatic test since it would relieve the technician of setting altitude levels manually.

AIRCRAFT ENGINE RPM INSTRUMENT TESTING

The GPIB automatic test system can be implemented into almost any test situation and is limited only by your imagination. An example of this is in the testing of aircraft engine rpm instruments which contain both digital and analog readouts, each of which display percentage rpm. A test sequence using the IEEE-488 bus can easily be designed, but it will require the interaction of a technician to provide the analog and digital readings as the test progresses. For a more automatic test sequence, it would be a simple

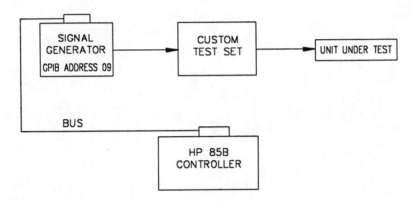

Figure 11-7.   Engine RPM instrument test setup.

matter to provide a test connector in the unit under test (space permitting) to report back to the controller the BCD logic levels fed to each digit of the display, but that would not check the readout devices themselves. For analog readings, an optical sensor which detects pointer position would be a very complicated and expensive device. Here we have a situation in which the technician and software can be effectively used to work together to enhance the GPIB implementation of an automatic test station.

In this application of the interface system a signal generator is used to provide a sine wave at selected frequencies to simulate the aircraft engine rpm frequencies to which the instrument responds. At each checkpoint the technician is instructed to read both displays of the unit under test and enter the data via the computer keyboard. The computer compares the data to the unit specifications which are stored in its memory and prints the results of the test and a pass or fail indication on the test data form.

In addition to the rpm test, the engine instrument was checked for response time. This measurement is readily made with the computer and technician working together, as shown in the program illustrated below. Figure 11-7 shows the test setup.

The controller in this test sequence was the Hewlett-Packard HP85B computer, and the signal generator was the Wavetek model 278 function generator set to GPIB address 09. A custom test set, connected between the signal generator and unit under test, provided the necessary power to drive the engine rpm instrument. Program 11-3, which follows, is the program that was used:

The following is an explanation of the steps of the Program 11-3:

Line 30 clears the Wavetek function generator to default status.

Line 40 establishes memory space in the computer for the variables in the program lines that follow.

Line 50 is a composite string which contains all of the frequency commands which will be used to set generator frequency.

Lines 60 through 90 contain the 13 checkpoints of the percentage rpm test which are stored in variable R(X).

Line 110 contains a string, A$, which is to be used for the display prompts to the technician.

Lines 160 through 180 set the function generator to the desired operating mode and disable its front panel keyboard.

Lines 200 through 310 are a FOR-NEXT loop which contains the 13 rpm checkpoints in which the technician is instructed to read the displays and enter the data into the computer via the keyboard. As each set of data is entered, the computer sets the frequency for the next test until all checkpoints are measured.

Lines 320 through 620 are the sequence which directs the computer to print the test results on the test data form. Note that any failure of the unit at any of the checkpoints is flagged.

```
10 ! ENGINE RPM INSTRUMENT TEST
20 CLEAR
30 CLEAR 709
40  DIM A$[29],F$[65],A(61),B(61),R(61)
50  F$="F00.0F07.0F14.0F21.0F28.0F35.0F42.
        0F49.0F56.0F63.0F70.0F72.8F77.0"
60  FOR X=1 TO 61 STEP 5
70  DATA 0,10,20,30,40,50,60,70,80,90,100,104,110
80  READ R(X)
90  NEXT X
100 A$="PRESS CONTINUE KEY WHEN READY"
110 DISP "THIS PROGRAM WILL CHECK ENGINE RPM INSTRUMENTS"
120 DISP A$
130 PAUSE
140 CLEAR
150 PRINT "ENGINE RPM TEST DATA"
160 REMOTE 709
170 LOCAL LOCKOUT 7
180 OUTPUT 709 ;"C0,B4,P0,U2.5,V2.5,D0,A5,F70.00"
190 OUTPUT 709 ;"I"
200 FOR X=1 TO 61 STEP 5
210 IF X>1 THEN 220 ELSE 270
220 OUTPUT 709 ;"P1I"
230 OUTPUT 709 ;F$[X,X+4]
240 DISP "RPM CHECK POINT = ";R(X)
250 OUTPUT 709 ;"I"
260 OUTPUT 709 ;"F"
270 DISP "TYPE IN DIGITAL AND ANALOG READINGS SEPARATED"
275 DISP "BY A COMMA"
280 DISP A$
290 INPUT D(X),A(X)
```

Program 11-3   *(continued)*

```
300 CLEAR
310 NEXT X
320 PRINT "TEST RESULTS"
330 PRINT "ANALOG DIAL"
340 PRINT USING "2X,3A,3X,4A,3X,5A"; "RPM","DIAL","ERROR"
350 FOR X=1 TO 61 STEP 5
360 IMAGE DDD.D,XX,DDD.D,XXX,DDDD.D
370 PRINT USING 360 ; R(X),A(X),A(X)-R(X)
380 NEXT X
390 PRINT "DIGITAL DIAL"
400 PRINT USING "2X,3A,3X,4A,3X,5A" ; "RPM","DISP",
                "ERROR"
410 FOR X=1 TO 61 STEP 5
420 PRINT USING 360 ; R(X),D(X),D(X)-R(X)
430 NEXT X
440 PRINT "THIS UNIT HAS FAILED THE FOLLOWING RPM"
445 PRINT "CHECKPOINTS"
450 PRINT "ANALOG DIAL"
460 Z=0
470 FOR X=1 TO 61 STEP 5
480 IF ABS (R(X)-A(X))>1 THEN 490 ELSE 510
490 PRINT R(X);TAB (8);A(X);TAB (17);A(X)-R(X)
500 Z=Z+1
510 NEXT X
520 IF Z>0 THEN 540 ELSE 530
530 PRINT "NONE"
540 PRINT "DIGITAL DISPLAY"
550 Z=0
560 FOR X=1 TO 61 STEP 5
570 IF ABS (R(X)-D(X))>1 THEN 580 ELSE 600
580 PRINT R(X);TAB (8);D(X);TAB (17);D(X)-R(X)
```

Program 11-3   *(continued)*

```
590 Z=Z+1
600 NEXT X
610 IF Z>0 THEN 630 ELSE 620
620 PRINT "NONE" @ GOTO 630
630 DISP A$
640 PAUSE
650 PRINT "RESPONSE TIME TEST"
660 CLEAR
670 DISP "RESPONSE TIME TEST"
680 REMOTE 709
690 LOCAL LOCKOUT 7
700 OUTPUT 709 ;"C0,B4,P0,U2.5,D0,F91.68,A5,I"
710 OUTPUT 709 ;"F"
720 DISP "PRESS CONTINUE KEY WHILE WATCHING POINTER"
730 DISP "WHEN POINTER REACHES 110% PRESS CONTINUE"
735 DISP "KEY AGAIN"
740 PAUSE
750 OUTPUT 709 ;"P1I"
760 T0=TIME
770 CLEAR
780 PAUSE
790 T1=TIME
800 CLEAR
810 PRINT "RESPONSE TIME =";T1-T0;" SECONDS"
820 IF T1-T0>1.5 THEN 830 ELSE 850
830 PRINT "UNIT FAILED RESPONSE TIME TEST" @ GOTO 860
840 CLEAR
850 PRINT "UNIT PASSED RESPONSE TIME TEST"
860 DISP "TEST IS COMPLETED"
870 END
```

Program 11-3

Lines 650 through 850 contain a response time test which uses the computer real-time clock (and technician) to measure the time required for the unit under test to respond to an abrupt change in input frequency. The result of this test is summarized on the test data form.

The Engine rpm test software described above contains some programming features which do not appear in the previously described applications. Note that in line 100 a string variable is used to display a much used phrase. This saves computer program memory. The same technique could be used when it is necessary to print a given phrase many times. Line 50 contains a complex string containing all GPIB commands which are to be sent to the function generator. Using a five-step FOR-NEXT loop allows line 230 to extract the desired command.

AIR DATA COMPUTER TEST

One of the most rewarding applications of the IEEE-488 automatic test system was realized in the testing of a complex air data computer which required a 3-hour QC verification check after the unit was fully adjusted and tested by a technician. The GPIB test setup reduced the time to about 40 minutes, automatically printed the QC report, and flagged any of the checkpoints that the unit under test did not pass. In addition to reducing QC test time to only one-quarter of what was previously required, it virtually eliminated disputes between the test and QC sections of the production department.

Figure 11-8 illustrates the test setup that was used. The controller for this automatic test station was the Hewlett-Packard model HP85B computer. The other instruments that were required were:

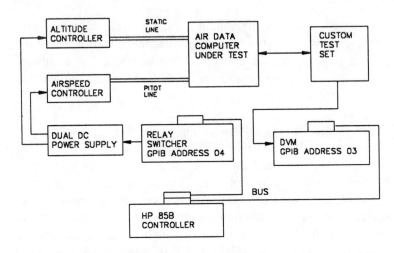

Figure 11-8.   Air data computer test setup.

1. Fluke model 8840A GPIB controlled digital voltmeter with
    a GPIB address of 03.
2. Two Mensor model 12275 precision pressure controllers,
    one to simulate altitude and the other to simulate airspeed.
    Each unit was remotely controlled by 0- to 5-volt analog dc
    source which provided the desired vacuum or pressure
    output.
3. A dual dc power supply, constructed in house, which con-
    tains analog circuitry which is externally controllable by
    relay closures. The power supply is used to generate two
    discrete dc voltages that are used to set the desired altitude
    and airspeed simulation of the test sequence.
4. ICS model 4874A GPIB controlled relay switcher which
    was used to contol the outputs of the power supply and direct
    the input of the voltmeter in accordance with the test se-
    quence. The relay switcher was assigned a GPIB address of
    04.

ALTITUDE	AIRSPEED						
	100	150	200	250	300	350	375
0	.002	.093	.182	.271	.358	.442	-
10K	.031	.136	.238	.336	.435	.527	.573
20K	.067	.189	.306	.416	.524	.627	.671
30K	.115	.255	.387	.511	.628	.729	-
40K	.173	.335	.484	.616	-	-	-
50K	.264	.456	.624	-	-	-	-

Figure 11-9.   Air data computer test data matrix.

5.   A custom test set to interface the air data computer with the digital voltmeter.

The actual software for the air data computer test required 592 program lines and is far too lengthy to be reproduced in its entirety here. Instead, the most informative and important sections are illustrated, and an analysis of the techniques involved in the test sequence are presented.

Figure 11-9 illustrates one of two test data specifications which had to be verified. These contain a matrix of six altitudes and seven airspeeds in which a voltage ratio, generated by the unit under test, had to be measured and verified to be within certain test limits. One test matrix was for ac voltage ratios; the other for dc. The ac and dc matrix represent a total of 66 individual ratio measurements that had to be made. To enter this data into the computer, a two dimensional variable was assigned. This was called $A(X,Y)$ for the ac voltage ratio, and $D(XY)$ for the dc ratio. The program sequence to store the ac data matrix into computer memory is:

```
240 FOR Y=1 TO 6
250 FOR X=1 TO 7
260 READ A(X,Y)
270 DATA .002,.093,.182,.271,.358,.442,0
280 DATA .031,.136,.238,.336,.435,.527,.573
290 DATA .067,.189,.306,.416,.524,.627,.671
300 DATA .115,.255,.387,.511,.628,.729,.0
310 DATA .173,.335,.484,.616,0,0,0
320 DATA .264,.156,.624,0,0,0,0
330 NEXT X
340 NEXT Y
```

Additional memory space was allocated for ac and dc ratio measurement data that would be assimilated and calculated by the computer. $B(X,Y)$, $C(X,Y)$, $E(X,Y)$, and $F(X,Y)$ variables were assigned for this purpose.

To simplify program lines, complex strings which were required to control the relay switcher and digital meter were defined in string variables such as K1$, M1$, and M2$. For example, three relays in the switcher, numbers 16, 17, and 18, had to be set in various combinations to simulate seven different airspeeds. A 0 placed after the relay number commanded that relay to open; a 1 caused it to close. String variable K1$ was defined as:

```
K1$=
"R160R170R180R161R170R180R160R171R180R161R171R180R160R170
R181R161R170R181R161R171R181"
```

This string provides all combinations of a 3-bit binary code which will cause the airspeed controller to automatically sequence through the seven airspeeds, as shown in the software illustrated below. The following program lines provided the automatic sequence in which the altitude was set to zero and seven airspeeds

were simulated so that the ac and dc ratios of the air data computer
could be measured:

```
1230 CLEAR 704
1240 CLEAR
1250 KEY LABEL
1260 DISP "ALTITUDE = 0 FEET";TAB (20);"AC";TAB (27);"DC"
1270 OUTPUT 704 ;"R151R131"
1280 OUTPUT 704 ;"R061"
1290 WAIT 15000
1300 FOR Y=1 TO 61 STEP 12
1310 X =(Y-1)/12+1
1320 OUTPUT 704 ;0$
1330 OUTPUT 704 ;K1$[Y,Y+11]
1340 OUTPUT 703 ;M2$
1350 OUTPUT 704 ;"R020R030R040R011"
1360 WAIT 5000
1370 ENTER 703 ; V
1380 OUTPUT 704 ; "R010R021"
1390 WAIT 5000
1400 ENTER 703 ; B(X,1)
1410 C(X,1)=INT (10000*B(X,1)/V+.5)/10000
1420 OUTPUT 703 ;M1$
1430 OUTPUT 704 ;"R010R020R040R031"
1440 WAIT 2000
1450 ENTER 703 ; V
1460 OUTPUT 704 ;"R030R041"
1470 WAIT 2000
1480 ENTER 703 ; E(X,1)
1490 F(X,1)=INT (10000*E(X,1)/V+.5/10000
1500 DISP K(X);"KNOTS";TAB (17);E(X,1);TAB (25);F(X,1)
1510 NEXT Y
```

The following is a discussion of the test sequence shown above:

Line 1230 clears the relay switcher so that all relays are opened.

Line 1260 displays the identity of the special function keys which may be used by the technician to abort a current test and run another out of the normal sequence of the program.

Line 1260 displays current altitude simulation of the test.

Lines 1270 and 1290 set relays 15, 13, and 6 of the relay switcher to preset the proper conditions, including zero altitude, for the test sequence to follow.

Line 1290 allows a 15-second waiting period to allow the airspeed and/or altitude simulators to settle down in the event that this test has been selected out of sequence by the technician.

Line 1300 begins a FOR-NEXT loop which will sequence the test through seven airspeeds, 0 through 375 knots.

Line 1310 converts the variable Y, which changes in steps of 12, to another variable X, which changes in steps of 1.

Line 1320 uses string variable O$ to clear relays 1, 2, 3, and 4 of the relay switcher.

Line 1330 selects the desired airspeed of the sequence, using string K1$ and variable Y to command the relay switcher to provide the proper 3-bit code to the airspeed power supply.

Line 1340 uses string variable M2$ to direct the voltmeter to assume ac voltage function at the desired range and reading rate.

Line 1350 causes relays 1, 2, 3, and 4 to connect the input of the voltmeter to the proper test point and set certain other conditions in the test set for the voltage ratio test to follow.

Line 1360 provides a 5-second delay to allow the unit under test to stabilize.

Line 1370 directs the voltmeter to transmit to the computer the magnitude of the ac driving voltage in the unit under test. This voltage reading is stored in variable V.

Line 1380 controls relays 1 and 2 and switches the voltmeter to a second test point in the unit under test.

Line 1380 provides a 5-second waiting period for the circuit to stabilize.

Line 1400 directs the voltmeter to transmit its reading to the computer, which stores it in variable $B(X,1)$.

Line 1410 computes the ratio output of the unit under test by dividing the voltage measurement of line 1400 by the measurement taken in line 1370. Note that this calculation is rounded to four decimal places and is stored in variable $C(X,1)$.

Line 1420 sets the voltmeter dc voltage function.

Line 1430 causes the relay switcher to connect the voltmeter to the appropriate test point in the unit under test in preparation for the dc voltage ratio to follow.

Lines 1440 through 1510 continue the dc measurement sequence in a similar manner as described for the ac voltage ratio test.

The above program is repeated six more times to cover the remaining six altitude points, making a total of 66 measurements. In each of those sequences the variables A, B, C, D, E, and F are assigned the value 2 through 6. For example, line 1400 above becomes ENTER 703; B(X,2) in the second test sequence. As each altitude sequence is performed, the computer displays the results on the CRT so that a technician monitoring the test can abort it if the results are not satisfactory.

The combinations of airspeed and altitude which are not required are easily deleted from any of the sequences by an appropriate selection of the range of variable Y in the FOR-NEXT loop. When the entire test is completed, the results are printed on the test data form and any points which are not within spec are flagged. The equipment automatically returns the unit under test to zero altitude and airspeed so that the next unit can be checked.

In the test setup described above several variations can be made, at higher cost, to simplify both the setup and software. For example, the use of four voltmeters can eliminate the requirement to physically switch one meter to four test points. Even two voltmeters could be used to advantage. Also, GPIB programmable vacuum/pressure test sets, to simulate each of the required altitudes and airspeeds, are available. The use of such components in the test setup could eliminate the custom designed power supply and relay switcher.

This automated test for an air data computer is able to run, completely unattended, once the technician connects the equipment and starts the sequence. About 40 minutes later the test is completed and the test data form can be reviewed to determine if the unit meets QC standards. The beauty of such a test setup is that while the test is being conducted, the technician can devote time to preparing the next unit for test or to perform other required duties. It doesn't take a mathematician to calculate the rapid payback time to cover the cost of the IEEE-488 instrumentation.

Appendix A

ASCII/ISO and IEEE
Code Chart

B7 B6 B5 →	0 0 0	0 0 1	0 1 0	0 1 1	1 0 0	1 0 1	1 1 0	1 1 1
BITS B4 B3 B2 B1	**CONTROL**		**NUMBERS SYMBOLS**		**UPPER CASE**		**LOWER CASE**	
0 0 0 0	0 NUL 0 0	20 DLE 10 16	40 SP 20 32	60 0 30 48	100 @ 40 64	120 P 50 80	140 ` 60 96	160 p 70 112
0 0 0 1	1 GTL SOH 1 1	21 LLO DC1 11 17	41 ! 21 33	61 1 31 49	101 A 41 65	121 Q 51 81	141 a 61 97	161 q 71 113
0 0 1 0	2 STX 2 2	22 DC2 12 18	42 " 22 34	62 2 32 50	102 B 42 66	122 R 52 82	142 b 62 98	162 r 72 114
0 0 1 1	3 ETX 3 3	23 DC3 13 19	43 # 23 35	63 3 33 51	103 C 43 67	123 S 53 83	143 c 63 99	163 s 73 115
0 1 0 0	4 SDC EOT 4 4	24 DCL DC4 14 20	44 $ 24 36	64 4 34 52	104 D 44 68	124 T 54 84	144 d 64 100	164 t 74 116
0 1 0 1	5 PPC ENQ 5 5	25 PPU NAK 15 21	45 % 25 37	65 5 35 53	105 E 45 69	125 U 55 85	145 e 65 101	165 u 75 117
0 1 1 0	6 ACK 6 6	26 SYN 16 22	46 & 26 38	66 6 36 54	106 F 46 70	126 V 56 86	146 f 66 102	166 v 76 118
0 1 1 1	7 BEL 7 7	27 ETB 17 23	47 ' 27 39	67 7 37 55	107 G 47 71	127 W 57 87	147 g 67 103	167 w 77 119
1 0 0 0	10 GET BS 8 8	30 SPE CAN 18 24	50 (28 40	70 8 38 56	110 H 48 72	130 X 58 88	150 h 68 104	170 x 78 120
1 0 0 1	11 TCT HT 9 9	31 SPD EM 19 25	51) 29 41	71 9 39 57	111 I 49 73	131 Y 59 89	151 i 69 105	171 y 79 121
1 0 1 0	12 LF A 10	32 SUB 1A 26	52 * 2A 42	72 : 3A 58	112 J 4A 74	132 Z 5A 90	152 j 6A 106	172 z 7A 122
1 0 1 1	13 VT B 11	33 ESC 1B 27	53 + 2B 43	73 ; 3B 59	113 K 4B 75	133 [5B 91	153 k 6B 107	173 { 7B 123
1 1 0 0	14 FF C 12	34 FS 1C 28	54 , 2C 44	74 < 3C 60	114 L 4C 76	134 \ 5C 92	154 l 6C 108	174	7C 124
1 1 0 1	15 CR D 13	35 GS 1D 29	55 - 2D 45	75 = 3D 61	115 M 4D 77	135] 5D 93	155 m 6D 109	175 } 7D 125
1 1 1 0	16 SO E 14	36 RS 1E 30	56 . 2E 46	76 > 3E 62	116 N 4E 78	136 ∧ 5E 94	156 n 6E 110	176 ~ 7E 126
1 1 1 1	17 SI F 15	37 US 1F 31	57 / 2F 47	77 ? 3F 63	117 O 4F 79	137 — 5F 95	157 o 6F 111	177 RUBOUT (DEL) 7F 127
	ADDRESSED COMMANDS	UNIVERSAL COMMANDS	LISTEN ADDRESSES		TALK ADDRESSES		SECONDARY ADDRESSES OR COMMANDS	

KEY:

octal **25** PPU — Message Mnemonic
NAK — ASCII/ISO character
hex **15 21** decimal

Appendix B

Mnemonics of the
IEEE-488 Interface System

AAD	Assign address	ESE	Event status enable
AH	Acceptor handshake	ESE?	Event status enable query
ATN	Attention	ESR?	Event status register query
C	Controller	EXE	Execution error
CAL?	Calibration query	GET	Group execute trigger
CLS	Clear status	GMC?	Get macro contents query
CME	Command error	GTL	Go to local
DAV	Data valid	IDN?	Identification query
DC	Device clear function	IFC	Interface clear
DCL	Device clear command	IST?	Individual status query
DDE	Device-dependent error	L	Listener
DDT	Define device trigger	LE	Extended listener
DDT?	Define device trigger query	LLO	Local lockout
DIO	Data input/output	LMC?	Learn macro query
DLF	Disable listener function	LRN?	Learn device setup query
DMA	Direct memory access	LU	Logical unit
DMC	Define macro	MAV	Message available bit
DT	Device trigger	MLA	My listen address
E	Drivers	MSS	Master summary status bit
EMC	Enable macro	MTA	My talk address
EMC?	Enable macro query	NDAC	No data accepted
EOI	End or identify	NRFD	Not ready for data
ESB	Event status bit	OPC	Operation complete

OPC?	Operation complete query
OPT?	Option identification query
PCB	Pass control back
PMC	Purge macros
PON	Power-on
PP	Parallel poll
PPU	Parallel poll unconfigure
PRE	Parallel poll enable register enable
PRE?	Parallel poll enable register enable query
PSC	Power-on status clear
PSC?	Power-on status clear query
PUD	Protected user data
PUD?	Protected data user query
QYE	Query error
RCL	Recall instrument state
RDT	Resource description transfer
RDT?	Resource description transfer query
REN	Remote enable
RL	Remote/local
RQC	Request control
RST	Reset
SAV	Save instrument state
SDC	Selected device clear
SESR	Standard event status register
SH	Source handshake
SPD	Serial poll disable
SPE	Serial poll enable
SR	Service request function
SRE	Service request enable
SRE?	Service request enable query
SRQ	Service request command
SRER	Service request enable register
STB?	Read status byte query
T	Talker
TCT	Take control
TE	Extended talker
TRG	Trigger
TST?	Self-test query
UNL	Unlisten
UNT	Untalk
URQ	User request
WAI	Wait to complete

Appendix C

Glossary of IEEE-488 Terms

Acceptor. Any device on the bus which can receive a message in command or data mode.

Address. A 7-bit code assigned to a GPIB device which allows it to be specifically addressed for talking or listening by the controller.

Addressed commands. Commands which allow the controller to cause specific actions from selected devices on the bus.

ASCII. American Standard Code for Information Interchange.

Asynchronous. The occurrence of an event which is not synchronized with the system clock rate.

ATE. Automatic test equipment. A group of GPIB instruments, together with the proper software, is considered an automatic testing system.

ATN control line. Used to distinguish between command mode and data mode for messages on the data I/O lines.

Bidirectional bus. A group of lines which can be used by any device for both receiving and transmitting.

Bit. The smallest part of a binary number which carries intelligible information.

Bit parallel. A set of concurrent data bits present on the signal lines of the bus.

Bus. A set of lines which are used in the interface system to carry messages and data.

Bus commands. ASCII codes which have useful meaning to devices on the bus and cause specific actions by them.

Byte. A binary word containing eight bits. In the GPIB system the eighth bit is often ignored since it is not needed in ASCII coding.

Byte serial. A system of sending a series of 8-bit words in succession to carry messages and data over the bus.

Command mode. When ATN is true (low), the devices on the bus may be addressed or unaddressed as listeners or talkers. Bus commands are also sent in this mode.

Compatibility. A property of GPIB devices which allows them to communicate with each other in the interface system.

Controller. A GPIB device which sets the ATN line and addresses all other devices as listeners and/or talkers. There can be only one active controller on the bus at any given time.

Data mode. When the ATN line is false (high), data or instructions are transferred between devices on the bus.

DAV. Data valid control line which is used in the handshake sequence.

Default. The operating status of a GPIB device upon power-up, as designated by the manufacturer. To change the default status, commands from the controller are required.

Device clear. ASCII character DC4 which causes all devices to return to the default state.

Device-dependent message. An addressed message sent on the bus which is directed to a specific device or instrument to cause a desired action.

DIO. Mnemonic which refers to the eight data input/output lines of the bus.

Direct memory access. A technique by which data may be directly transferred into the memory bank of a controller or computer without the need for READ and WRITE software commands as required in the normal GPIB data transfer sequence.

EOI. End or identify control line of the bus which is used to indicate the end of a series of data bytes in a message; it is also used in the parallel poll.

Extended listener. A GPIB instrument which is capable of being assigned a secondary listen address.

Extended talker. A GPIB instrument which is capable of being assigned a secondary talk address.

Go to local. ASCII character SOH which will cause all addressed listeners to return to local control.

GPIB. General purpose instrumentation bus.

Group execute trigger. ASCII character BS which initiates simultaneous actions by addressed listeners.

Handshake. A sequence of events on the NRFD, DAV, and NDAC lines which ensures that each data byte is properly received by the intended recipient.

High state. A logic 1 level which, in the GPIB system, indicates a not true condition.

HP-IB. Hewlett-Packard Interface Bus.

IEEE. Institute for Electrical and Electronic Engineers.

IFC. Interface clear management line used by the controller to halt all current operations, unaddress devices, or disable serial poll.

Interface. A boundary between one part of a system and another through which information is transferred.

Listener. A device on the bus which has been addressed to receive data or instructions from the controller or other instruments.

Local control. A condition in a GPIB device which permits settings and adjustments by means of its front or rear panel controls.

Local lockout. A GPIB universal command, ASCII character DCI, which disables the manually operable controls (other than power on/off) of an instrument.

Low state. A logic 0 level which, in the GPIB system, indicates a true condition.

LU. Mnemonic for logical unit.

MLA. My listen address which, in a given GPIB device, allows it to be enabled to listen.

Mnemonic. A shortened form or abbreviation of a term or expression which is used as a system of memory assistance or training.

MTA. My talk address which, in a given GPIB device, allows it to be enabled to talk.

NDAC. No data accepted control line used in the handshake sequence.

NRFD. Not ready for data control line used in the handshake sequence.

Parallel poll. A method by which the controller can simultaneously check the status of eight or more instruments on the bus.

Primary commands. A group of multiline messages consisting of universal commands, addressed commands, and device addresses sent by the controller when ATN is true.

Programmable. The capability of an instrument or device which allows it to be set, adjusted, or controlled, usually by the controller in a GPIB system.

Query. A message sent from the controller to an instrument to elicit desired information. A query takes the form of a header followed by a question mark.

Remote control. A method by which a device is directed to perform its intended tasks through instructions from the controller.

REN. Remote enable line of the bus which allows instruments to respond to commands from the controller or another talker.

Secondary commands. A group of multiline messages which allow extended talkers and extended listeners to respond to 2 address bytes, or parallel poll enable and disable.

Selective device clear. ASCII character EOT which returns addressed devices to their default state.

Serial poll. A method by which the controller can sequentially check the status of all instruments on the bus. Each instrument can send back an 8-bit word to the controller.

Serial poll disable. ASCII character EM which, when sent in command mode, will cause the bus to go out of serial poll mode.

Source. A talker on the bus.

Signal. A single state or series of logical states on any line of the bus.

System. An interconnection of two or more GPIB devices which is designed to perform a designated task.

SRQ. Service request control line which allows a device on the bus to alert the controller that it requires service.

Talker. A GPIB device which transmits data to the bus, either in response to an addressed command from the controller or asynchronously.

Unidirectional bus. A group of lines which is used by an individual device for one-way (input or output) transfer of information.

Unlisten. A command from the controller which causes a GPIB listener to ignore messages.

Untalk. A command from the controller which causes a GPIB talker to cease talking.

Universal command. A command sent by the controller to all devices on the bus, whether or not they are addressed.

Word. A single or group of bytes treated as a unit of information.

Appendix D

Minimum IEEE-488.2 Device Capabilities

SOURCE HANDSHAKE (SH)

SH0 No Capability

SH1 Full Capability

ACCEPTOR HANDSHAKE (AH)

AH0 No Capability

AH1 Full Capability

TALKER

Talker (T) Extended Talker (TE)

	Basic Talker	Serial Poll	Talk Only Mode	Unaddress if MLA
T(TE)0	NO	NO	NO	NO
T(TE)1	YES	YES	YES	NO
T(TE)2	YES	YES	NO	NO
T(TE)3	YES	NO	YES	NO
T(TE)4	YES	NO	NO	NO
T(TE)5	YES	YES	YES	YES
T(TE)6	YES	YES	NO	YES
T(TE)7	YES	NO	YES	YES
T(TE)8	YES	NO	NO	YES

LISTENER

Listener (L) Extended Listener (LE)

	Basic Listener	Listen Only Mode	Unaddress if MTA
L(LE)0	NO	NO	NO
L(LE)1	YES	YES	NO
L(LE)2	YES	NO	NO
L(LE)3	YES	YES	YES
L(LE)4	YES	NO	YES

SERVICE REQUEST (SR)

SR0 No Capability

SR1 Full Capability

REMOTE LOCAL (RL)

RL0 No Capability

RL1 Complete Capability

RL2 No Local Lockout

PARALLEL POLL (PP)

PP0 No Capability

PP1 Remote Configuration

PP2 Local Configuration

DEVICE CLEAR (DC)

DC0 No Capability

DC1 Full Capability

DC2 Omit Selective Device Clear

DEVICE TRIGGER (DT)

DT0 No Capability

DT1 Full Capability

DRIVER ELECTRONICS (E)

E1 Open Collector (250 KB/sec max)

E2 Tri State (1 MB/sec max)

CONTROLLER (C)

There are 29 controller levels. The more significant are:

C0 No Capability

C1 System Controller

C2 Send IFC and Take Charge

C3 Send Ren

C4 Respond To SRQ

C5 Send Interface Messages, Receive Control, Pass Control, Pass Control to Self, Parallel Poll, Take Control Synchronously

Appendix E

IEEE-488.2 Common Commands and Queries

*AAD, Accept Address. Allows the controller to detect all address configurable devices on the bus, then assigns an IEEE-488.1 address to each.

*CAL?, Calibration. Tells a device to perform an internal self-calibration, which must be accomplished without any local user interaction. The device will respond to this query with a number in the range of -32767 to 32767. A value of 0 in the response indicates that the calibration was carried out successfully.

*CLS, Clear Status. Clears the status register and status data structures which are summarized in the status byte. It also clears all status-related queues except the output queue.

*DDT, Define Device Trigger. Stores one or more device commands which are to be executed when the IEEE-488.1 GET message or 488.2 TRG command is sent.

*DDT?, Define Device Trigger. Allows the user to read the command sequence which will be followed when a device receives the GET or *TRG command.

*DLF, Disable Listener Function. Tells a device to stop listening on the bus in preparation to being configured with the *AAD command.

*DMC, Define Macro. Allows the user to assign a series of commands which the device is to execute upon receipt of the macro label. The macro is defined by sending DMC followed by a string that designates the label. Following the label, the user sends an arbitary block program data element which defines the macro.

*EMC, Enable Macro. Enables and disables macros, without affecting macro definitions. The command is followed by a number in the range of -32767 to 32767. A zero disables all macros; a number other than zero enables them. Macros may be disabled when it is desired to send a device-dependent command which is the same as the macro label.

*EMC?, Enable Macro. Permits the user to determine if macros are enabled in a device. The unit will respond with a value of 1 (ASCII 49 decimal) or 0 (ASCII 48 decimal) to indicate if the macros are enabled or disabled, respectively.

*ESE, Standard Event Status Enable. This command, followed by a number in the range of 0 to 255, will set the Standard Event Status Enable register bits. The binary equivalent of the number represents the values of the individual bits set into the SESE register.

*ESE?, Event Status Enable. Enables the user to read the contents of the Standard Event Status Enable register. The device will return a number in the range of 0 to 255, whose binary equivalent represents the bits of the SESE register.

*ESR?, Event Status Register. Enables the user to read the contents of the Standard Event Status register, which is automatically cleared. The device responds with an integer in the range of 0 to 255. The binary equivalent of the integer represents the bits of the SESR.

*GMC?, Get Macro Contents. This query, followed by the label string of the macro, allows the user to obtain the contents of the macro in a device.

*IDN?, Identification. Causes a device to respond with its identity. The returned data is organized into four fields, separated by commas. The unit must respond with its manufacturer and model number and may also report its serial number and options. If the latter information is not available, the device must return an ASCII 0 (decimal 48) for each.

*IST?, Individual Status. Permits the user to read the current state of the ist local message of a device. It permits the user to determine what the device will send on a parallel poll, without performing the poll.

*LMC?, Learn Macro. Tells a device to respond with the labels of all currently defined macros, whether or not they are enabled. If there is more than one macro label to report, they will be separated by a comma.

*LRN?, Learn Device Setup. Tells a device to send a response that contains all the neceesary commands to set the device to its present state. This information is used by the controller to learn how to restore at a later time an instrument that has been manually set up.

*OPC, Operation Complete. Causes a device to set bit 0 in the Standard Event Status register when it completes all pending operations.

*OPC?, Operation Complete. Causes a device to place an ASCII 1 (decimal 49) in its output queue when it completes all pending operations.

*OPT?, Option Identification. Allows the user to determine the identity of any reportable device options. The device response must not be longer than 255 characters and may contain any number of fields separated by commas. The format is left up to the manufacturer of the equipment, with missing options identified by an ASCII 0 (decimal 48). Fields describing the options may contain any ASCII characters except commas, semicolons, control characters, and DEL.

*PCB, Pass Control Back. Instructs a potential bus controller where to pass control back to. The current controller can tell another device where to send the 488.1 TCT command when it is ready to relinquish control of the bus. The TCT command is followed by a number which represents the address of the next controller of the bus.

*PMC, Purge Macros. Removes all macro labels and sequences from a device's memory.

*PRE, Parallel Poll Enable Register Enable. This command, followed by a number in the range of 0 to 65535, sets the bits in the Parallel Poll Enable register. The binary equivalent of the number represents the bits in the PPER.

*PRE?, Parallel Poll Enable Register Enable. Allows the user to read the contents of the Parallel Poll Enable register. The device responds with an integer in the range of 0 to 65536, whose binary equivalent represents the bits of the PPER.

*PSC, Power-on Status Clear. This command, followed by a number in the range of -32767 to 32767, is used to control the power-on clearing of the Service Request Enable register, the Standard Event Status Enable register, and the Parallel Poll Enable register. Sending a number other than zero sets the power-on clear flag true, causing the registers to be cleared at power-on and preventing the device from requesting service.

*PSC?, Power-on Status Clear. Enables the user to read the status of the power-on clear flag. The device returns a 0 or 1, indicating that the flag is false or true, respectively.

*PUD, Protected Data User. Enables the user to store in a device's memory up to 63 bytes of data, such as calibration date, usage time, or any other information unique to the device. The data is protected by some means such as a hidden switch so that it can only be written when the protection mechanism is disabled.

*PUD?, Protected User Data. Reads the data stored by the *PUD command, allowing the user to access this information.

*RCL, Recall Command. This command restores the state of a device to a status previously stored in the device's memory. If the device has more than one memory register, the command must be followed by a number to specify which register is to be used. The functions restored by the *RCL command are the same as those affected by the *RST command.

*RDT, Resource Description Transfer. Allows the user to store a capability description in a device's memory. The data is protected by some means such as a hidden switch so that it can only be written when the protective mechanism is disabled.

*RDT?, Resource Description Transfer. Allows the user to access the Resource Description stored by the *RDT command.

*RST, Reset. Sets device-dependent functions to a known state, sets the Device Defined Trigger to a device defined state, disables macros, purges all *OPC commands and queries, and aborts all pending operations. The output queue, Service Request Enable register, Standard Event Status Enable register, and power-on flag are not affected.

*SAV, Save. Allows the user to store the present state of a device in local memory. If the device has more than one memory location, the command must be followed by a number to designate the storage register to be used.

*SRE, Service Request Enable. This command, followed by a number, sets the Service Request Enable register which determines what bits in the status byte will cause a service request from the device. The binary equivalent of the number represents the values of the individual bits of the SRER.

*SRE?, Service Request Enable. Enables the user to read the contents of the Service Request Enable register. The device returns a number in the range of 0 to 63 or 128 to 191, since bit 6 (RSQ) cannot be set. The binary equivalent of the number represents the value of the bits of the SRER.

*STB?, Status Byte. Reads the status byte containing the master summary status (MSS) bit. The device responds with an integer in the range of 0 to 255, whose binary equivalent represents the value of the bits of the status byte.

*TRG, Trigger. This IEEE-488.2 command performs the same function as the Group Execute Trigger command defined by IEEE-488.1.

*TST?, Self-Test. Tells a device to perform an internal self-test and report back to the controller if any errors are detected. The response sent by the device will be a number in the range of -32767 to 32767. A zero in the response indicates that no errors were detected.

*WAI, Wait to Continue. Causes a device to wait until all previous commands and queries are completed before executing any which follow the *WAI command.

Appendix F

IEEE-488.2 Floating-Point Format

The IEEE-488.2 document recommends that IEEE Std. 754-1985 be used for representing floating-point numbers in the GPIB system. The specified format requires that each number be represented by three fields, Sign, Exponent, and Fraction. The size of the fields depends upon the desired precision of the number. For single and double precision numbers the size of the fields are shown in Figure A-F1.

SINGLE PRECISION 32 BIT NUMBER		
Sign field width	1	bit
Exponent field width	8	bits
Fraction field width	23	bits

DOUBLE PRECISION 64 BIT NUMBER		
Sign field width	1	bit
Exponent field width	11	bits
Fraction field width	52	bits

Figure A-F1

The following formulas may be used to determine the value of a number x represented in IEEE 754 floating-point format. Let e represent the exponent, s the sign bit, and f the fraction. A 32-bit single-precision number is determined by

If $e = 255$ and $f \neq 0$ then x is Not a Number (NaN)
If $e = 255$ and $f = 0$ then $x = -1^s (\infty)$
If $0 < e < 255$ then $x = -1^s (2^e - {}^{127})(1 = f)$
If $e = 0$ and $f \neq 0$ then $x = -1^s (2 - {}^{126})(0 = f)$
If $e = 0$ and $f = 0$ then $x = -1^s (0)$ (zero)

Figure A-F2

A 64-bit double-precision number is determined by

If $e = 2047$ and $f \neq 0$ then x is Not a Number (NaN)
If $e = 1047$ and $f = 0$ then $x = -1^s (\infty)$
If $0 < e < 2047$ then $x = -1^s (2 \, {}^{-1023})(1 + f)$
If $e = 0$ and $f \neq 0$ then $x = -1^s (2-1022)(0 + f)$
If $e = 0$ and $f = 0$ then $x = -1^s (0)$ (zero)

Figure A-F3

Figure A-F4 is a representation of the relationship of the bits in a single-precision number, shown as a 4-byte transmission.

Figure A-F5 is a representation of the relationship of the bits in a double-precision number, shown as an 8-bit transmission.

8	7	6	5	4	3	2	1	
S	E_{msb}	E	E	E	E	E	E	First byte sent
E_{lsb}	F_{msb}	F	F	F	F	F	F	Second byte sent
F	F	F	F	F	F	F	F	Third byte sent
F	F	F	F	F	F	F	F_{lsb}	Fourth byte sent

Where:
E_{msb}	is the most significant bit of the exponent.
E_{lsb}	is the least significant bit of the exponent.
F_{msb}	is the most significant bit of the fraction.
F_{lsb}	is the least significant bit of the fraction.
S	is the sign bit.
E	is an exponent bit.
F	is a fraction bit.

Figure A-F4

Note that the numbers illustrated above will be sent as a *length arbitrary response data* and received as an *arbitrary block program data*.

8	7	6	5	4	3	2	1	
S	E_{msb}	E	E	E	E	E	E	First byte sent
E	E	E	E_{lsb}	F_{msb}	F	F	F	Second byte sent
F	F	F	F	F	F	F	F	Third through seventh byte send
F	F	F	F	F	F	F	F_{lsb}	Last byte sent

Where:
E_{msb}	is the most significant bit of the exponent.
E_{lsb}	is the least significant bit of the exponent.
F_{msb}	is the most significant bit of the fraction.
F_{lsb}	is the least significant bit of the fraction.
S	is the sign bit.
E	is an exponent bit.
F	is a fraction bit.

Figure A-F5

Appendix G

Electrical Specifications of the IEEE-488 Interface System

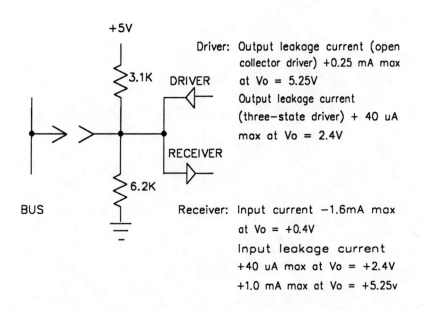

+5V

3.1K   DRIVER

RECEIVER

6.2K

BUS

Driver: Output leakage current (open collector driver) +0.25 mA max at Vo = 5.25V
Output leakage current (three-state driver) + 40 uA max at Vo = 2.4V

Receiver: Input current −1.6mA max at Vo = +0.4V
Input leakage current +40 uA max at Vo = +2.4V
+1.0 mA max at Vo = +5.25v

Appendix H

Mechanical Specifications of the IEEE-488 Interface System

The IEEE/ANSI connector and cabling specifications of the IEEE-488 Interface System permit interconnecting all devices together in a star or linear configuration. The IEEE-488/ANSI connector is a 24-pin ribbon-type connector, and the IEC 625.1 connector is a 25-pin type connector (MIL-C-24308). The pin assignments of the IEEE/ANSI connector are shown in Figure A-H1.

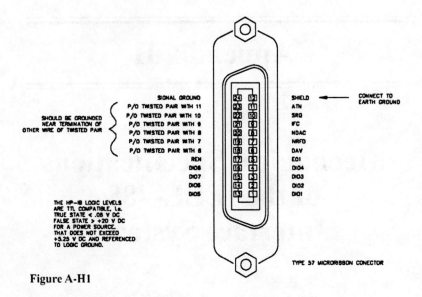

Figure A-H1

Specifications for the IEEE/ANSI connector are:

Voltage rating: 200 Vdc
Current rating: 5 amperes
Endurance: 1000 insertions
Temperature and humidity: MIL STD 202E

Specifications for the IEC 625.1 connector are:

Voltage rating: 60 Vdc
Current rating: 5 amperes
Endurance: 1000 insertions
Temperature and humidity: IEC publication 68 for climatic
category 25/070/21

For the IEEE/ANSI connector, metric threads (ISO M3.9 x 0.6
type) are specified, but some existing assemblies use English

threads. Typically, metric threads are colored black; English are colored silver. No attempt should be made to mate English and metric threads together. To do so will damage the hardware.

Appendix I

Sample GPIB Programming Sequences Using HP-BASIC

SERIAL POLL

The following program is an example of the use of the serial poll. In this sequence a Fluke model 8840A digital voltmeter (GPIB address 15) is continuously polled by the computer to determine if the instrument is experiencing an overrange condition.

```
10 CLEAR
20 OUTPUT 715 :"N1P1"
30 LOCAL 715
40 S=SPOLL (715)
50 IF BIT (S,0)=1 THEN 70
60 GOTO 40
70 DISP "OVERRANGE"
80 GOTO 10
```

Program A-11   Serial poll.

Line 20 sets the SRQ mask of the digital meter. P1 programs the 8840A to make a service request on the condition specified by the integer following the N command. In this case, the integer 1 causes the instrument to generate an SRQ when in an overrange condition. Other integers following the N command could be used to set certain other operating conditions, as specified by the manufacturer of the instrument.

Line 30 sets the DVM to local operation, allowing use of the front panel controls by the user.

Line 40 causes the computer to transmit a serial poll, addressed specifically to the DVM, to determine if an SRQ has been asserted by that instrument.

Line 50 checks the serial poll register of the DVM to determine if bit 1, defined as bit 0 in the HP85B computer, has been asserted. If this bit is at logic 1 level, the program branches to line 70. Otherwise the program returns to line 40 to transmit another serial poll.

```
100 ON TIMEOUT 7 GOTO 170
110 SET TIMEOUT 7;1200
120 OUTPUT 715 ;"R1F1S0T4"
130 TRIGGER 715
140 ENTER 715 ; A
150 DISP A
160 GOTO 130
170 DISP "INTERFACE FAILURE"
180 FOR I=0 TO 6
190 STATUS 7,I ; S(I)
200 DISP "STATUS BYTE #";I;" = ";S(I)
210 NEXT I
220 RESET 7
230 GOTO 130
```

Program A-I2   Time-out.

If the instrument has asserted the overrange bit, line 70 of the program causes the computer CRT to display the word OVER-RANGE, and the process is repeated.

TIME-OUT

Program A-I2 illustrates the use of the computer time-out feature, which is a very useful function that can be used to avoid the problem of interface bus hang-ups when a command or data transfer sequence is not properly completed. In this example, an interface problem may be simulated by turning off the addressed device, a Fluke digital voltmeter set to GPIB address 15.

The following explains pertinent steps in Program A-I2:

Line 100 specifies the program line for a subroutine which the computer is to follow in the event the time-out function is exercised.

Line 110 sets the time limit for a handshake sequence to be completed; in this case it is specified as 1200 milliseconds, or 1.2 seconds.

Lines 120 programs the voltmeter to the 200 mv-range, dc volts, slow reading rate, and external trigger mode.

Line 130 commands the voltmeter to take a voltage reading.

Line 140 directs the voltmeter to transmit the reading to the controller, which stores it into variable A.

Line 150 displays the voltage reading on the computer CRT. The sequence is repeated as long as the time to complete any message or data transfer does not exceed 1.2 seconds.

If a bus hang-up is simulated by turning off power to the voltmeter so that it cannot complete the handshake sequence, the program branches to line 170, which displays INTERFACE FAILURE on the computer CRT.

A FOR-NEXT loop is initiated which causes the computer to store a set of interface status bytes in variable S(I). The CRT then displays the results of the status bytes, which are defined by the manufacturer of the controller. A typical display would look like this:

```
INTERFACE FAILURE
STATUS BYTE # 0 = 1
```

```
STATUS BYTE # 1 = 0
STATUS BYTE # 2 = 66
STATUS BYTE # 3 = 0
STATUS BYTE # 4 = 53
STATUS BYTE # 5 = 226
STATUS BYTE # 6 = 0
```

The HP IEEE-488 interface instruction manual provides information concerning the cause of failure of the system.

Line 220 resets the bus so that a new message or data transmission may take place. If the problem causing the hang-up has not been corrected, the sequence of lines 170 through 220 is repeated.

In an actual program, the software engineer would provide the desired action that the controller is to follow when the branch statement of line 100 is exercised. The subroutine must cause the desired action, either by manual or automatic means, to allow the automatic test sequence to proceed.

COMBINATION SERIAL POLL AND TIME-OUT

It is possible to use the two sequences described above in a novel program which automatically determines the address of every device on the bus. The following program also makes use of a command which enables the sequence to continue in the event of a programming error. In this case the error occurs when the controller attempts to conduct a serial poll on itself.

The following explains pertinent steps in Program A-I3:

Line 100 sets the time-out limit to 500 milliseconds.

Line 110 directs the program sequence to a subroutine at line 210 in the event of a program error.

```
100 SET TIMEOUT 7;500
110 ON ERROR GOTO 210
120 ON TIMEOUT GOTO 180
130 FOR I=0 TO 31
140 X=SPOLL (700+I)
150 DISP "DEVICE ADDRESS # ";I;" PRESENT"
160 NEXT I
170 END
180 ABORTIO 7
190 DISP "DEVICE ADDRESS # ";I;"NOT PRESENT"
200 GOTO 160
210 OFF ERROR
220 GOTO 160
```

Program A-I3   Combination serial poll and time-out.

Line 120 directs the program sequence to a subroutine at line 180 in the event of a bus hang-up.

Lines 130 through 160 form a FOR-NEXT loop which is used to query every possible device address for a response to the serial poll. The decimal value of the status byte returned, if any, is stored in variable X which, in this program, is not used for any purpose. If a status byte is received, the computer displays the variable I and indicates that the device is present and active on the bus.

If a device at any of the addresses queried does not exist, the branch statement of line 120 is invoked, since no reply is forthcoming within the allotted time of 500 milliseconds. This causes the computer to display the address of all devices which are not present, and it indicates this fact.

Since this program will query all GPIB addresses from 0 to 31, the controller itself will be polled because it has a factory- set GPIB address of 21. The attempt of the controller to perform a serial poll on itself will normally cause a program error and stop the sequence. This problem has been eliminated, however, by taking advantage of the ON ERROR statement which allows the sequence to branch to a subroutine. The program sequence then returns to the next GBIB address to be polled. Note that the computer CRT will indicate the presence or absence of all devices except address 21, which is the controller.

MANUAL ACTIVATION OF SRQ

Some instruments or devices feature a front panel pushbutton or switch which enables the technician to manually request service from the controller. This can be a very useful operating control as shown in the following program, which permits a series of meter readings to be displayed and stored on the computer CRT. The DVM for this example is the Fluke model 8840A which is set to a GPIB address of 15.

The following explains pertinent steps in Program A-I4:

Lines 100 to 130 clear the computer screen, interface, and set the digital voltmeter to default functions.

Line 130 sets the conditions under which the SRQ line will be asserted by the meter. N4 provides SRQ on activation of the front panel SRQ pushbutton, P1 is the "put" command to set the SRQ

```
100 CLEAR
110 CLEAR 7
120 CLEAR 715
130 OUTPUT 715 ;"N4P1Y1"
140 LOCAL 715
150 ON INTR 7 GOTO 500
160 ENABLE INTR 7;8
300 GOTO 300
500 CONTROL 7,1 ; 0
510 X=SPOLL (715)
520 IF X<> 0 THEN 530 ELSE 140
530 ENTER 715 ; A,A$
540 DISP A,A$
550 ENABLE INTR 7;0
560 GOTO 140
570 END
```

Program A-I4   Manual activation of SRQ.

mask, and Y1 enables the output suffix (VDC) to be transmitted with the numeric data.

Line 140 sets the meter to local front panel control.

Line 150 commands the controller to branch to line 500 in the event of an SRQ interruption.

Line 160 enables the interface for an interrupt when SRQ is true.

The program then sequences to line 300, which simulates controller activity with other matters. The program will remain at line 300 until SRQ is asserted by the user.

Lines 500 through 560 form a subroutine which is exercised at the activation of the SRQ front panel pushbutton. The DVM is polled by the controller, and if the serial poll register is not zero, a voltage reading is stored in variable A and the suffix VDC is stored in A$.

Line 540 displays the results on the computer CRT and the program cycles back to line 140 to repeat the sequence and wait for the next SRQ.

INSTRUMENT INTERROGATION

Many instrument manufacturers have provided a method of interrogating an instrument to determine specific information concerning its status or capabilities. For example, the Wavetek model 278 function generator, when equipped with a memory backup battery, is able to store up to 100 complex settings which can be recalled at any time. This feature is very useful since it eliminates the necessity of setting each parameter of the instrument every time it is powered up. This function generator has been implemented with a talk function which allows a GPIB controller to determine the precise settings which have been stored in the instrument's memory.

Program A-I5 will determine the number of settings which the generator is capable of storing and will display the complete command string of each setting that is stored. The GPIB address of the function generator is 09.

```
100 CLEAR
110 DIM S$[100],T$[100],Z$[100]
120 Y$="Y"
130 OUTPUT 709 ;"XT8"
140 ENTER 709 ; S$
150 DISP S$
160 FOR Z=0 TO 99
170 Z$=VAL$ (Z)
180 T$=Y$&Z$
190 OUTPUT 709 ;T$
200 OUTPUT 709 ;"I"
210 OUTPUT 709 ;"XT3"
220 ENTER 709 ; S$
230 DISP Z;S$
240 NEXT Z
250 END
```

Program A-I5   Instrument interrogation.

The following explains the pertinent steps in Program A-I5.

Line 110 dimensions three string variables which will be used to store alphanumeric data provided by the generator.

Line 130 contains the command which instructs the generator to respond with the number of stored settings when it is addressed to talk.

Line 140 directs the generator to transmit this information, and the computer stores it in string variable S$ which is displayed on the computer CRT.

Lines 160 through 240 form a FOR-NEXT loop which will recall and interrogate the generator for its stored settings 100 times.

Line 170 defines string Z$ which is the numeric value of variable Z.

Line 180 uses the concatenation operation of the computer to construct the device dependent command from lines 120 and 170.

Lines 190 and 200 command the generator to recall and execute the stored setting for the current value of Z.

Line 210 instructs the generator to respond, when addressed to talk, with the current setting as defined in line 190.

Line 220 commands the generator to transmit this information to the computer, which stores it in string S$. This is displayed on the screen.

This program will execute in just a few seconds, and the generator display will change too fast for the human eye to follow. If desired, a wait statement may be added after line 200 to allow the generator display to remain stable for the ongoing process to be seen.

DATA TRANSFER USING FAST HANDSHAKE

The following program makes use of the fast handshake capability of the HP 85B computer to transfer large amounts of data that may be assimilated by a GPIB instrument. In this example, the extremely fast measurement capability of a Fluke model 8840A digital voltmeter (100 readings per second) is transferred and stored by the computer using the fast handshake (FHS) data transfer.

```
100 CLEAR
110 CLEAR 715
120 OUTPUT 715 ;"F1R3S2"
130 ENTER 715
140 DIM A$[1308]
150 IOBUFFER A$
160 TRANSFER 715 TO A$ FHS ; COUNT 1300
170 FOR X=1 TO 1300 STEP 13
180 DISP (X-1)/13+1;A$[X,X+11]
190 NEXT X
200 END
```

Program A-I6   Data transfer using fast handshake.

Lines 100 and 110 clear the computer CRT and sets the digital voltmeter to default functions.

Line 120 sets the DVM to the 20 volt DC range at a rate of 100 readings per second.

Line 130 addresses the meter to talk.

Line 140 allocates sufficient space in the computer's memory to store the data which is to be transferred. Eight characters of the string variable A$ are reserved for control of HP85B buffer activity and 13 characters are required for each data byte of the DVM.

Line 150 specifies that string variable A4 will be transferred to the I/O buffer.

Line 160 is the fast handshake command which directs the DVM to transfer 100 readings into string variable A$. Note that each data byte of the meter contains 13 characters and the transfer continues until a total of 1300 characters have been transferred. During the fast handshake sequence, the computer suspends program execution and dedicates itself to the task of moving all the characters from the interface into the buffer. Once the fast handshake transfer begins no interrupts are allowed, and the computer will see the transfer through to completion.

The data transfer has now taken place, and 100 voltage readings are stored in string variable A$. The total amount of elapsed time is about 1 second. Lines 170 through 190 form a FOR-NEXT loop which can be used to display the stored readings on the computer CRT, each preceded by a number from 1 to 100.

Bibliography

1. Byers, TJ, *Electronic Test Equipment*, Intertext Publications/McGraw-Hill, New York, 1987.
2. Hughes, W. and Luehman, K., "PCIB: A Low-Cost, Flexible Instrument Control for Personal Computers," *Hewlett-Packard Journal*, May, 1986.
3. Kane, G., Harper, S., and Ushijima, D., *The HP-IL System: An Introductory Guide to the Hewlett-Packard Interface Loop*, Osborn/McGraw Hill, New York, 1982.
4. Tilden, M. "Tektronix Codes and Formats for GPIB Instruments," Tektronix, 1982.
5. Tilden, M. "Programming Techniques Speed IEEE-488 System Execution," *EDN*, October 27, 1983.
6. "Tutorial Description of the Hewlett-Packard Interface Bus," Hewlett-Packard publication 5952-0156 revised November 1987.

Index

Trademarks

Wavetest is a trademark of Wavetek, Inc.

Tektronix is a trademark of Tektronix, Inc.